THE PENGUIN BOOK OF SAUCES

Ambrose Heath, culinary journalist, author and broadcaster, was born in Hampstead in 1891 and was educated at Clifton College. Before the First World War, whilst preparing to write, he lived in Newlyn. He then moved to London, where he remained until 1932. He was a regular contributor to the *Guardian* and to the *Daily Mirror*, where he was responsible for the cookery strip 'Patsy' and for the 'Digwell' strip. He was cookery correspondent for the *Morning Post*, now defunct, and the *Yorkshire Post*, and contributed to such magazines as *Queen*, *Ideal Home* and *Housewife*. Wireless fans knew him for his 'Kitchen Front' during the Second World War. A very prolific writer, whose distinctive style has been much commented on, he was the author of *Learn to Cook by Pictures*, 1960, *The Queen Cookery Book*, 1960, *Hay Box Cookery*, 1961, *The Bird's Eye Book of Britain's Favourite Recipes*, 1964, and more recently, *Meat*, 1968. Mr Heath, who was married, died in 1969.

AMBROSE HEATH

The Penguin Book of
SAUCES

PENGUIN BOOKS

Penguin Books Ltd, Harmondsworth, Middlesex, England
Penguin Books Inc., 7110 Ambassador Road, Baltimore, Maryland 21207, U.S.A.
Penguin Books Australia Ltd, Ringwood, Victoria, Australia

—

First published 1970
Reprinted 1973

—

Copyright © The Estate of Ambrose Heath, 1970

—

Made and printed in Great Britain by
Cox & Wyman Ltd,
London, Reading and Fakenham
Set in Monotype Bembo

Contents

Introduction

The Penguin Book of Sauces is Ambrose Heath's last contribution to
cookery literature: he died, having completed the book to its proof
stage without, however, having had time to write an introduction.
Yet a book on sauces does need an introduction, for no part of
culinary procedure is likely to arouse more controversy, historical
speculation or fierce patriotism than these deceptively simple-
sounding 'garnishes'.

According to Larousse, we understand by sauce 'in a general way
every kind of liquid seasoning for food'. This hardly sounds appetiz-
ing, and anyway neither 'garnish' nor 'seasoning' even begins to do
justice to this mysterious element which, alone, is responsible for the
present pre-eminence of French cuisine. 'Sauces are the splendour
and glory of French cooking,' says Julia Child in *Mastering the Art of
French Cooking* 'yet there is nothing secret or mysterious about making
them.'

This, fortunately, is quite true – provided always that one has a
fairly firm grasp of the basic principles. For initial encouragement
one should know that really there are only six 'mother sauces', and
that even these divide quite neatly into two distinct families deriving
their respective characters from two simple processes which require
no more skill than can be acquired in three or four attempts by even
the most left-handed cook.

One group is based on the roux process: a thickening ingredient
obtained through cooking flour and fat together to a perfect blend.
A lightly-cooked roux is the basis for two white sauces, one in
which the liquid used is milk-based producing a mother sauce called
Béchamel, and one which uses stock-based liquid resulting in a
Velouté. If the roux is cooked until it becomes a rich nut-brown
colour and then used with a stronger, darker stock the result is a basic
brown sauce usually termed Espagnole and in its extreme form
Demi-glace. Red sauces are made with tomato or red wine, and it is

of course possible to make green sauces using vegetable stock: these variations, however, are aesthetic only and do not alter the basic process.

The second family of sauces is formed by emulsion, and again includes three mother sauces. Two of them use egg yolks as their active ingredient. For Hollandaise the yolks are warmed, flavoured with lemon juice, and beaten with butter; for Mayonnaise they can be used cold, and instead of butter, oil is beaten in. The third member of this family we know as a dressing rather than a sauce: it is the Vinaigrette, made with oil and vinegar.

Flavoured butters, both hot and cold (the latter also known as hard sauces) form a less important and much smaller separate group.

These six (or seven) basic formulas, then, are nothing but the working principles, the mechanics, in creating a sauce. The really important ingredient is the stock – in French rightly known as the *fond de cuisine*. A good stock can be created out of choice ingredients, or can happen out of left-overs – in daily practice, it will more frequently do the latter, and that is only right and proper because, paradoxically, the present almost embarrassingly-rich catalogue of French sauces is a direct result of a decaying economy.

During the Middle Ages 'sauce' was usually one of two things: a heavy, rich gravy made of simmered-down meat stock and herbs, or a sweet coating obtained from honey or cane sugar with vinegar and a variety of spices: the true forerunner of the present *chef saucier* is the caramelist. Even in the days of Louis XIV a *sauce béchamel* was still a much-enriched simmering of milk, veal and seasonings which might take days to prepare, but in the century that followed the country's exhausted economy (as well as the rising *cuisine* of the parsimonious bourgeoisie) turned to the quicker and cheaper roux which had first been introduced by the Spanish cooks of Anne of Austria.

That is the second paradox of the *grandes sauces* of French cooking: their basic processes are all foreign imports – the roux from Spain, the Hollandaise from the Low Countries, and the Mayonnaise (after Mahón, on once-French Menorca) from common Mediterranean practice. The one all-important ingredient which France added to all of them was simply imagination.

And that, we think, is the spirit in which the making of sauces should be approached: get to know the basic processes absolutely backwards, and use the recipes in this or any other book as guidelines only. For the rest: imagination – and, hopefully, taste. No matter what the purists say: there is more satisfaction in creating a sauce of your own, than in weighing the ingredients for somebody else's . . .

Selection of Sauces for Certain Dishes

SAUCES FOR MEAT

Grilled Meat

Chilli 2
Crapaudine
Devil 1, 2
Devilled
Finiste
Garlic
Gherkin 1
Gubbins
Henriette

Kidney
Sauce au Beurre d'Anchois
Sauce Béarnaise
Sauce Bordelaise 1, 2
Sauce Chateaubriand
Sauce Paloise
Sauce for Steak
Toulouse

Beef

Barbecue
Brown Mushroom 1, 2
Fluffy Mustard
Grapefruit
Gratin
Green Ranchero
Sauce Bourguignonne
Sauce Chasseur
Sauce Chateaubriand
Sauce Diable 1, 2
Sauce Godard

Sauce Italienne 1
Sauce Piquante
Sauce Provençale 1, 2
Sauce for Roast Beef
Sauce Robert
Sour 2
Sour Cream
Spanish
Vinaigrette 2
Wyvern

Boiled Beef

Bourgeoise
Chives 2, 3
German
Gherkin 2

Grapefruit
Horseradish 1, 2, 5, 6
Horseradish with Currants
Horseradish Hollandaise

Olive 1
Sauce Belle Créole
Sauce Italienne 1

Sauce Pimprenelle
Sauce for Boiled Beef
Savoury Mustard

Veal

Anchovy
Apple and Horseradish 1–3
Bacon
Brown Almond
Cider
Cucumber 3
Green Ranchero
Hungarian
Pimento
Pimento and Green Pepper
Sauce Allemande

Sauce au Porto
Sauce Chasseur
Sauce Hongroise
Sauce Ivoire
Sauce Villageoise
Sauce Zingara 1, 2
Sauce for Roast Veal
Sorrel 1, 2, 3
Spanish
Tunny Fish
Veal Gravy Tomatée

Mutton

Apple 2
Barbecue 2
Currant Jelly
Fennel 2
Grapefruit
Portarlington
Prune 2

Sauce au Porto
Sauce Italienne
Sauce for Boiled Mutton
Sauce for Roast Mutton
Sauce for Steak
Spanish

Lamb

Barbecue 2
Bread 1–4
Brown Mushroom
Brown Wine
Currant Jelly
Gherkin 2
Gooseberry 2
Gratin
Green 2
Littleton
Mint 1, 2

Onion 1
Orange Mint
Pickled Walnut
Red-Currant Mint
Sauce Bonnefoy
Sauce Chasseur
Sauce Choron
Sauce Diable 1, 2
Sauce Godard
Sauce Marquise
Sauce Piquante

Sauce Provençale 1, 2
Sauce Robert
Sauce Suédoise
Sauce Zingara 1, 2
Savoury Cream

Savoury Mustard
Vinaigrette 2
Walnut Gravy
Walnut 1

Pork

Apple and Horseradish 1-3
Christopher North's
Orange 6
Oxford
Prune 1
Sage and Onion
Sauce Charcutière

Sauce Nantaise
Sauce Robert
Savoury Cream
Sour 2
Sour Cream
Sultana

Ham or Tongue

Champagne
Cider
Cumberland 2
Colony Club
Fluffy Mustard
Grape Juice
Olive 1

Oxford
Raisin 1-4
Sauce Madère
Sauce for Ham
Savoury Cider
Sour Cream
Yorkshire

Sucking-Pig

Currant 1
Prune 1, 2

Sultana

Sheep's Head

Brain

Calf's Head

Michael Kelly's
Michael Kelly's Sharp
Sauce Ravigote 1, 2
Sauce Tortue

Sauce for Calf's Head 1, 2
Tartare
Vinaigrette 1

Boiled Fowl

Alexandra
Almond 4
Cauliflower
Chestnut 2
Celery
Cucumber 3
Lemon 2
Liver 1, 2

Liver and Parsley
Oyster 1, 2, 3
Sauce Albuféra
Sauce à l'Estragon 1, 2
Savoury Custard
Tarragon 2
Watercress

Roast Chicken

Augolemon
Bacon
Bread 1–4
Brown Almond
Chervil
Chestnut
Cranberry and Apple
Cranberry and Celery
Egg 2
Green 2
Horseradish 4

Littleton
Milk Gravy
Montebello
Mousseline 1
Mushroom 2
Peanut Butter
Russian
Sauce Suprême
Sorrel 1–3
Tarragon 3
Vegetable Sauce

Duck

Cranberry 2
Christopher North's
Gooseberry 3
Ham
Olive 2
Orange 4, 5, 6
Sage and Onion

Sauce aux Cerises
Sauce Bigarade
Sauce Rouennaise 1, 2
Sauce for Goose or Duck
Sauce for Wild Duck
Yorkshire

Goose

Apple 1
Christopher North's
Gooseberry 3

Sauce aux Cerises
Sauce for Goose or Duck

Selection of Sauces for Certain Dishes

Turkey

Almond 3, 4
Chestnut 2
Cranberry 1

Cranberry and Celery
Oyster 3

Wild Duck

Hanoverian
Orange 1, 3
Sauce Bigarade

Sauce Infernale
Sauce for Wild Duck
Wine 3

Rabbit

Lemon 2
Liver 2
Liver and Parsley

Sauce for Boiled Rabbit
Sauce for Roast Rabbit

Hare and Venison

Alsatian
Chestnut 3
Cumberland 1
Jelly Wine
Oxford
Pickled Walnut
Portarlington
Port Wine
Prune 2

Sauce aux Cerises
Sauce aux Pignons
Sauce de la Vieille Charlotte
Sauce Grand-Veneur
Sauce for Hare
Sauce for Roast Hare
Sauce for Venison 1, 2
Venison

Other Game

Balbirnie
Basil
Bread 1–4
Cranberry 2
Cream 2
Game
Grapefruit
Ham
Horseradish 4
Jelly Wine
Orange 1, 3, 4, 6

Oxford
Portarlington
Port Wine
Richelieu
Sauce Appétissante
Sauce Diane
Sauce au Porto
Sauce Petit-Maître
Sauce for Cold Game
Vinaigrette 1
Wyvern

SAUCES FOR FISH

Boiled or Poached Fish

Almond 1
Béchamel Mayonnaise
Bloater
Caper 1, 2
Cockle
Crab 1, 2
Crab-Meat
Cucumber
Dill 1, 2
East India Mayonnaise
Eel
Egg 1
Fennel 1
Figaro
Gherkin 3
Genovese 1, 2
Golden Malaga
Green 1
Herring
Horseradish Hollandaise
Lemon 1
Lobster Hollandaise
Maître d'Hôtel 1, 2
Mussel
Neapolitan

Olive-Almond
Onion 2
Oyster 1, 2
Peg Woffington
Pimento-Parsley
Pineapple Cream
Rio Grande
Roe
Sauce Albert
Sauce Allemande
Sauce Amiral
Sauce Aurore 2
Sauce aux Herbes
Sauce Bavaroise
Sauce Belle Créole
Sauce Écossaise 1, 2
Sauce Landaise
Sauce Mousseline Dijonnaise
Sauce Mousseuse
Sauce Newburg
Sauce Souchet
Sauce Vin Blanc
Sour 1
Walnut 2
White Wine

Baked Fish (sometimes stuffed)

Beer Sauce
Dutch 1, 2
Figaro

Olive-Almond
Shallot
Sour 1

Grilled or Fried Fish

Chilli 2
Devil 1, 2
Finiste

Fish 5
Golden Malaga
Horseradish Hollandaise

Selection of Sauces for Certain Dishes

Sauce à l'Huile Provençale
Sauce Bordelaise 1
Sauce Épicurienne

Mousseline Dijonnaise
Walnut 2

Fish Salad

Almond 2
Chilli Mayonnaise
Fluffy Cucumber

Ravigote Mayonnaise
Savoury Mayonnaise

Fresh-Water Fish

Caper 2
Dutch 2
Horseradish 5

Sauce Canotière
Sauce Matelote
Wine 1

Herrings

Mustard 1, 2, 3

Mackerel

Fennel 1

Gooseberry 1, 4

Mullet, Red

Wine 2

Salmon

Caper 3
Chives Mayonnaise
Cucumber
Cucumber Hollandaise
Custard
East India Mayonnaise
Fennel 1

Horseradish 4
Indian 2
Mousseline 2
Sauce Matelote
Sauce Vin Rouge
Wine

Salt Cod, Boiled

Egg 1

Fried
Garlic 2

Sea Bream
Beetroot   Shallot

Sole, Turbot, Whiting

Lobster 1, 2   Sauce Grillon
Lobster Hollandaise   Sauce Marguéry
Oyster 1, 2   Sauce Newburg
Russian Oyster   Sauce Orientale
Sauce Cardinal 1   Sauce Victoria
Sauce Colbert   Sauce for Sole 1, 2

Lobster

Anisette   Sauce Newburg
Chives Mayonnaise   Sauce Orientale
Fluffy Cucumber   Sauce Russe
Russian   Sauce Victoria
Sauce Cardinal 1

Oysters
Sauce des Halles

MISCELLANEOUS

Eggs
Butter   Sauce Indienne
Cheese 1, 2   Sauce Mornay
Cream 1   Sauce Mousseline Dijonnaise
Mushroom 1   Sauce Normande 1
Normandy   Tomato Cheese
Parsley   Tomato Cream
Pimento-Parsley

Selection of Sauces for Certain Dishes

Macaroni and Pasta

Frontier
Garlic and Tomato
Genovese 1

Ragú alla Bolognese
Sauce aux Noix
Sugo

Vegetable Salad

Cream Cheese Mayonnaise
Mayonnaise (whisked)
Mustard Cream Mayonnaise
Pickle Mayonnaise
Pimento Mustard Mayonnaise

Piquant Mayonnaise 2
Ravigote Mayonnaise
Savoury Mayonnaise
Thousand Island Dressing

Asparagus

Asparagus
Asparagus Mayonnaise
Creamy Egg
Crumb

Sauce Bruxelloise
Sauce Maltaise
Savoury

Fruit Salad

Banana Nut Mayonnaise
Cheese Mayonnaise
Cream Cheese Mayonnaise

Honey Cream Mayonnaise
Marmalade Mayonnaise

Equivalent Measures

ENGLISH AND AMERICAN

A standard English measuring-cup holds 10 liquid ounces – that is, ½ pint (imperial measure), whereas an American measuring cup holds 8 liquid ounces, an American ½ pint. When dry ingredients are measured in a cup their weight (avoirdupois) will obviously vary with their density. A table showing some equivalent measures in American cups is given below.

1 pound flour (16 oz. avoirdupois) – 4 cups sifted flour
½ pound granulated and castor sugar – 1 cup
½ pound brown sugar – 1¼ cups
½ pound butter – 1 cup

When spoon measurements are given, the spoons are rounded, that is, they have as much above the bowl of the spoon as below.

METRIC

1 pint – approx. ½ litre
1 ounce – approx. 28 grammes
1 pound – approx. 450 grammes

First Principles and Basic Sauces

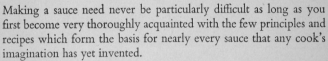

Making a sauce need never be particularly difficult as long as you first become very thoroughly acquainted with the few principles and recipes which form the basis for nearly every sauce that any cook's imagination has yet invented.

One thing that all sauces (and a good many soups) have in common is that they need a binding ingredient to hold the liquid and provide the required texture. This binding ingredient can be obtained in two very different ways.

THE ROUX PRINCIPLE

This is by far the most common, and at the same time also the easiest. Basically, a roux is a mixture of flour and butter, capable of binding more than half a pint of liquid for every ounce of its own weight. There are three different kinds of roux (known as white, blond and brown) but their preparation varies only in the time it takes to cook them. The ingredients are the same for all three kinds: just flour and butter, the latter outweighing the former by a small margin. The thickness of the sauce depends directly on the amount of flour per pint of liquid – roughly, one ounce per pint will result in a medium-thick general-purpose sauce, and one and a half ounces per pint in a fairly thick one. In level measures, use the same amount of butter.

WHITE ROUX

White roux is made by melting butter gently in a heavy saucepan and then stirring in the flour either off the fire or on a very low flame. As soon as the flour is fully stirred in, the roux is theoretically ready for use – but in this stage it would have a raw and pasty flour taste which disappears if the roux is cooked for a few more minutes. Take care that it does no more than froth slightly if you need a true white roux.

BLOND ROUX

Cook the roux a little harder and longer, until it turns an even straw colour.

Three of the great mother sauces are made on the basis of these light roux. The first and probably the oldest of these is

BÉCHAMEL SAUCE (White Sauce)

1 pint milk; white roux from 1½ oz. flour; 6 peppercorns; a pinch of salt; quarter of a medium-size onion; bouquet of parsley, thyme and bayleaf.

Add the onion, herbs and seasoning to the milk and heat on a low flame for about ten minutes; do not boil. Strain, then add slowly to the white roux, stirring all the while, and taking care to obtain a smooth blend every time some more liquid has been added. The first quarter is the critical stage, this had best been done off the fire. When the first quarter or third of the liquid has gone in and the blend is smooth, the pan can be returned to low heat and the rest of the liquid added more quickly. Keep stirring until boiling, boil for a few minutes, check the seasoning. Leave to simmer for at least half an hour to make sure the floury taste completely disappears (if the sauce is used first as a basis for another recipe, the cooking should take place after the other ingredients have been added).

VELOUTÉ SAUCE (White Sauce)

1 pint white stock (fish, meat or vegetable); blond roux from 1½ oz. flour; salt; pepper.

The stock should be of good quality, carefully strained, and completely free of fat. It is heated and then added to the freshly-made roux in the manner described above. After the sauce has boiled for a few minutes, it should be ready for use (provided the roux and the stock were well prepared) but it improves tremendously by being simmered for at least an hour, preferably an hour and a half. During this time it may be necessary to skim the sauce from time to time, and this is easier if the pan in which it is made is tall rather than wide, or if the pan is tilted slightly while the sauce is cooking (use an old metal spoon or something similar). If used on its own, add some lemon juice just before serving.

Velouté is also the basis for an enriched variant which has itself become one of the most used mother sauces:

SAUCE PARISIENNE or SAUCE ALLEMANDE

1 pint thick Velouté (made as above, but with a roux from 2 oz. flour instead of 1½); 3 egg yolks; ¼ pint cream.

Blend the egg yolks and the cream together by beating with a whisk, then beat in about a quarter of the sauce (which has first been heated) a little at a time. When this is done, the rest of the sauce can be added somewhat more quickly, or the egg mixture can be added to the sauce and slowly brought to the boil. Boil for 1 or 2 minutes, check seasoning (salt, pepper, lemon juice).

Common enrichments for white sauces are either butter (which should be beaten in shortly before serving, about an ounce to a pint for a basic sauce and up to three or four ounces for a very rich sauce like some fish sauces) or cream (added little by little to a very thick sauce at simmering point, a quarter of a pint or more to a pint of sauce, depending on the consistency you want to end up with). Sauces enriched with butter should be served immediately, otherwise the butter releases itself from suspension and floats on top. For the same reason butter should not be used in sauces with cheese, or in those which are to cover food which will be gratinéed.

BROWN ROUX

This is made in the same way and from the same proportions as white and blond roux, but the flour is cooked in the fat until it is an even nut-brown colour. The choice of fat, however, is wider: if the end result is to be a fine sauce, use clarified butter (melted and decanted to leave behind those milky substances which might render the fat bitter before it is brown), but for an ordinary sauce pork fat serves equally well, and even oil can be used. Fat in which vegetables have been cooked can also be used to great effect.

The basic sauce made on a brown roux base is known as

ESPAGNOLE SAUCE

1 pint brown stock (see p. 32); brown roux from 1 ½oz. flour; the mirepoix obtained from the recipe on p. 36.

Heat the stock and add it to the roux in the manner described under Béchamel Sauce; bring to the boil, then add the mirepoix and leave to simmer on as low a fire as possible for about three hours, skimming from time to time as described under Velouté Sauce. Especially during the last hour the clarification process can be helped along by adding a very small amount of cold stock to the sauce and then allowing it to come to the boil briefly before skimming. Do this two or three times. After three hours the sauce should be rubbed through a sieve before it is used either on its own or as a base for other sauces. If it is to be kept, stir occasionally while it cools to prevent a skin from forming on the top.

HALF-GLAZE SAUCE (Demi-glace)

This is the final perfection of the Espagnole: it is simmered even longer, skimmed yet more thoroughly, and finally has a tablespoonful of meat jelly (p. 33) added to it.

To make Half-Glaze with tomato add a third of its volume of Tomato Sauce (p. 170) to the ordinary Demi-glace.

A much quicker version of Espagnole Sauce is a simple Brown Sauce:

BROWN SAUCE

1 onion; 1 small carrot; 1 oz. butter or dripping; 1 oz. flour; ½ pint stock or water.

Cut the onion and carrot into pieces and brown them in the butter or dripping with the flour. Moisten with the stock or water, simmer for ten minutes, season to taste and serve. Many cooks colour this sauce with browning, but this should be unnecessary as it should get all the browning it requires from the frying of the vegetables. A pinch of sugar is sometimes added to help this process.

THE EMULSION PRINCIPLE

This is the foundation of two more families of sauces and it should be mastered before you embark on your own variations. Both are based on the process which takes place when egg yolks are forced to absorb a quantity of fat and to hold it in suspension. The difference between the two groups of sauces is in the particular kind of fat used (butter or oil).

HOLLANDAISE SAUCE

8 oz. butter; 3 egg yolks; 1 tbs. cold water; 1 tbs. lemon juice; good pinch of salt; pepper

Melt all but two half-ounce pieces of the butter over a low flame and set it aside. Put the egg yolks in a heavy saucepan (never use an aluminium one as this might discolour the sauce) and whisk them until they become thick, about one minute. Add water, lemon juice and salt; whisk for another minute. Add one of the half-ounce pieces of butter and put the pan into a bain-marie or on a very low flame (use an asbestos mat if your saucepan is on the thin side). Whisk again until it becomes a smooth thick cream. This is the most difficult stage of the operation, but as long as you heat the sauce slowly and gently nothing should go wrong: it is only sudden heat which curdles the yolks, and over-cooking which scrambles them. When the sauce forms a smooth light cream on the wires of the whisk the danger is past and you can take the pan off the fire. Beat in the second piece of butter. Keep beating the sauce and pour in the melted butter as slowly as possible, drop by drop, until the sauce becomes thick and creamy. Then add the rest in a thin trickle. When all the butter is in the sauce check the seasoning (salt, pepper and lemon juice).

It is quite possible to make Hollandaise in a liquidizer, but two things should be remembered: since the yolks cannot be cooked, the butter should be as hot as possible (but added just as slowly, which is easiest in a liquidizer with a drip feed top), and about half the amount of butter should be used because otherwise the sauce just clogs the liquidizer. More butter can be added by hand, again very slowly: the maximum amount one egg yolk will hold is nearly four ounces, but it is best not to go over three.

MAYONNAISE SAUCE

3 egg yolks; 1 tbs. lemon juice or wine vinegar; ½ tsp. salt; ½ tsp. dry mustard; ½ pint olive or salad oil; 1 tbs. boiling water

Beat the egg yolks in a mixing bowl until they are thick, which takes about one minute (the beating can be done by hand with a whisk or with an electric beater). Add the lemon juice, salt and mustard, and beat for another minute. Keep beating and start to add the oil, drop by drop. As long as you do not stop beating the mixture longer than to change hands, there is no real danger-point in this process. After a third of the oil has been added, you can speed up and add the rest in a thin stream, or have a rest. When all the oil is absorbed, beat in a tablespoonful of boiling water to prevent the sauce curdling; check the seasoning (salt, pepper, lemon juice).

Mayonnaise can also be made in a liquidizer, but it will be a bit lighter, and you must substitute one whole egg for the three yolks. The maximum amount of oil that one egg yolk will hold in suspension is a little over a quarter of a pint.

There is one other group of sauces which uses the emulsion principle, but here the oil is held in very temporary suspension in vinegar alone. The basic sauce of this group is the Vinaigrette.

VINAIGRETTE SAUCE (French Dressing)

1 part wine vinegar; 3 parts olive oil or good tasteless salad oil; salt (not more than ½ tsp. to a pint); a pinch dry mustard

Beat the vinegar with the salt and mustard in a mixing bowl until the salt is dissolved. Then slowly add the oil, beating all the while. When left standing the oil will float to the top again, but this can be remedied as often as necessary by vigorous beating.

THICKENINGS (Liaisons)

Apart from the usual method of using butter and flour which is generally well-known, there are three main ways of thickening a sauce: with kneaded butter (beurre manié), with potato flour, cornflour or arrowroot, and with egg yolk. Another method, thickening with blood, is suitable only for game.

KNEADED BUTTER (Beurre manié)

This is a simple mixture of raw flour and butter, used for quick thickening at the end of cooking. The proportions are two thirds of an ounce of flour and just a little more of butter. The two ingredients are incorporated with a fork until they form a smooth paste. This is then divided into pieces the size of a haricot bean to ensure that it mixes well with the liquid. Bring the sauce to the boil and add the pieces all at once, shaking the pan at the same time so as to amalgamate all together, and taking it off the heat now and then. The sauce should simmer very gently after the addition of the beurre manié and should not be allowed to boil again.

POTATO FLOUR or ARROWROOT

It is better to use arrowroot (or cornflour) instead of potato flour as they are finer flours, less is needed, and the result is just as good. Put a teaspoonful of the flour into a cup and add two tablespoonfuls of cold water by degrees, stirring with a wooden spoon all the time. When the sauce is boiling on a good heat add the flour all at once, while stirring the sauce with the other hand. It only takes a few seconds to do the trick.

EGG YOLK

Mix an egg yolk smoothly with a little cold liquid and add by degrees three or four tablespoonfuls of the hot sauce. Keeping the sauce off the heat, add the liaison a little at a time, stirring with a wooden spoon. Then put the pan back on the heat and stir gently until the liquid actually boils. Many people, indeed most, will tell you that it is wrong to boil a sauce thickened with egg yolk, but this is not so if the sauce contains flour. Indeed, it is important that it does boil, as much to prevent the taste of rawness as to make certain that the liaison is complete.

BLOOD

The best known way of using this thickening is with sauces for game. It is unlikely that you will ever be in a position to use blood from a freshly killed animal, but in this case it would be advisable to add a little vinegar to the blood while it is warm, to prevent it from clotting. If it comes from a dead animal there are sure to be clots in it, and these should be broken down with a fork and the blood very finely sieved just before use. Gently warm a quarter of a pint of the sieved blood and add it, by degrees, to several tablespoonfuls of the sauce. This mixture is then added to the hot sauce, off the heat, while a whisk is employed to mix all together. Then put the pan on a very gentle heat and simmer gently for two or three minutes.

STORAGE AND REPAIR

ROUX-BASED SAUCES

Keep hot in a bain-marie or over steam until needed, or refrigerate. Float a film of melted butter over the top of the sauce to prevent a skin forming.

If the sauce is lumpy, force it through a fine sieve, then simmer it. If it goes thin (through loss of flour in the sieving, or from the preparation itself) it can be restored either by reducing it over moderate heat while stirring constantly or by the addition of a thickening agent (p. 28). Too thick a sauce can be thinned with milk (Béchamel) or stock (Velouté), stirred in little by little.

HOLLANDAISE SAUCE

Keep warm (but not hot) in a bain-marie or on a well shielded small flame, like the pilot light of a cooker. It will hold for about an hour. Using the minimum amount of butter in the preparation, and beating the rest in just before serving makes it easier to keep the sauce, as does the addition of a small amount of white sauce. Hollandaise can be stored for several days in a refrigerator, or it can be deep frozen. To use after a long storage, beat a small amount over a very low heat or in a bain-marie, then beat the rest in little by little.

MAYONNAISE SAUCE

Keep in the smallest possible bowl, covered closely to prevent the formation of a skin. Refrigerate if it is to be kept for more than a few hours, but do not stir the sauce before it is back to room temperature, or it may turn. Turned Mayonnaise, or Mayonnaise which refuses to thicken in preparation, can be repaired by whisking a small amount with half a teaspoon of mustard until the mixture thickens. Then beat in the rest, little by little, and make sure each addition thickens before you go on. If the sauce is too thick beat in some more vinegar or lemon juice.

Stocks and Other Basic Ingredients

BROWN STOCK

3 lb. shin of beef; 2 lb. shin of veal; 4 oz. carrots; 4 oz. onions; blanched green bacon rind; bouquet of parsley, thyme and bayleaf; small clove garlic; pepper and salt; butter.

Ask the butcher to cut the meat from shin of beef and shin of veal and to break up the bones as small as possible. Put the meat aside while you chop up the carrots and onions and put them into a large stewpan with some blanched green bacon rinds, the bones arranged on top. Add half a pint of water and cook on a low heat, covered, until the water is completely reduced. Now add six pints of boiling water, and put in the bouquet, garlic, a pinch of pepper, and a good pinch of salt for each pint of water. Bring to the boil and simmer gently for at least five hours, making sure that the level of the liquid is kept up by the addition of more boiling water now and then.

When this stock is ready, gently brown the pieces of meat kept aside in butter in a saucepan, add half a pint of the stock, and reduce the liquid completely over a moderate heat. Repeat this twice, then add the rest of the stock and bring to the boil, skimming if necessary. Partly cover the pan and cook on slowly for another three hours. Strain through a fine sieve, let it get quite cold, and remove the fat from the surface. Use this glaze as required.

VEAL STOCK (Brown)

4 oz. onions and 2 oz. carrots cut in medium thick rings; few blanched rinds of green bacon, first boiled for about five minutes; 3 lb. shin and shoulder of veal (boned); 5 pints brown stock (above); bouquet of parsley, thyme and bayleaf.

Spread the onions, carrots and bacon rind in a heavy saucepan and on this bed put the veal and bones, cut up small. Pour over half a pint of the stock and let it boil away completely, then add the rest of the stock and the herbs. Partly cover the pan and put it on the lowest heat possible, then bring to the boil and simmer for three hours, when it is ready to strain into a bowl and be kept until wanted.

The meat and bones may be re-used for meat jelly (below), after being boiled again for a couple of hours and reduced again to a syrupy consistency, as already mentioned at the end of brown stock.

JUS LIÉ

The words Jus lié will often be found in French cookery books. This is made from a partial reduction of veal stock bound with arrowroot and is used in many dishes. For example, four pints of veal stock is reduced by half and thickened with two ounces of arrowroot, first mixed smoothly with a little cold stock. Cook for one minute and strain.

WHITE STOCK

5 lb. shin of veal (with some shoulder); ½ oz. salt; bouquet of parsley, thyme and bayleaf; 1 clove; ¼ lb. carrots; ¼ lb. onions; 1 medium leek; ¼ small head celery.

The meat should be boned and tied up, and the bones broken up and placed with the meat in five to six pints of cold water with the salt, and brought to the boil. It is then skimmed carefully, the herbs and vegetables are added, and it is cooked on a low heat for about two and a half hours. It is then strained finely into a bowl and kept until required.

CHICKEN STOCK

Add the giblets and carcass of a chicken to the above.

MEAT JELLY OR GLAZE

This is simply a reduction of brown or white stock which is strained successively through fine muslin into smaller saucepans, and skimmed carefully all the time until the jelly acquires a syrupy consistency and coats the back of a spoon shinily.

It is used mainly to finish various sauces, as will be discovered in the following pages, and adds to their lightness and depth of flavour when used sparingly. The first part of the process of reduction can be quite fast, but in the final stages it must be carried out as gently and slowly as possible.

FISH STOCK (Court-bouillon)

(To make 2 quarts)

2 lb. chopped raw fish bone (sole or whiting) or trimmings; 2 oz. minced onion; several sprigs parsley; 12 black peppercorns; juice of ½ lemon; ¼ bottle dry white wine.

Put the fish bones or trimmings into a buttered saucepan with the minced onion, parsley, peppercorns and lemon juice. Cover and let this stew for a while, shaking the pan every now and then. Now moisten with the white wine, take the lid off and let the liquid reduce by about half. Add two quarts of cold water, bring to the boil and leave to cook on a moderate heat for *twenty minutes* only. This is just the right amount of time to extract the aromatic and gelatinous properties from the bones; longer stewing will only impair the flavour of the stock. Strain through a conical sieve.

FUMET

Fumet is made in the same way as court-bouillon but it is stronger and the liquid is well reduced. It can be made from vegetable, fish, poultry or game.

FISH STOCK 2 (with Red Wine)

Fish stock is not usually made with red wine in the domestic kitchen, since the stock usually emerges from the ingredients of the dish. It is thought advisable for the sake of completeness, however, to give a recipe here, and few can better Escoffier's, which is based on the same theories and directions as the white fish stock described above.

2 lb. fish bones, heads and trimmings; 6 oz. minced onion; 1½ oz. parsley stalks; 1 bayleaf; 2 small sprigs thyme; 2 cloves garlic; 1 bottle red wine.

Put all the ingredients mentioned above into a tall thick-bottomed saucepan with two pints of water; bring to the boil, skim carefully, and cook for twenty to thirty minutes on a moderate heat. Then strain into a basin and use as required. Some mushroom parings, at the cook's discretion, may be added.

FISH GLAZE

The same principle is applied to fish stock as to meat stock (p. 32): it is reduced, after straining, to a thick glaze.

DUXELLES (Dry)

1 tbs. equal parts butter and olive oil; 1 tsp. chopped onion; 4 tbs. mushroom stalks and parings; salt and pepper; grated nutmeg; chopped parsley.

Lightly fry the chopped onion in the butter and olive oil. Add to this the mushroom stalks and parings, washed, chopped and pressed as dry as possible in a cloth. Stir all together over a quick heat until all the moisture has completely evaporated, then season with salt, pepper and grated nutmeg. Finally mix in thoroughly a coffeespoonful of well chopped parsley. Keep in a small basin covered with a piece of buttered greaseproof paper.

MARINADE

In certain recipes for meat and game the mixture in which the pieces have been marinated, the marinade, plays an important part in the making of the sauce, for example, Sauce Poivrade (p. 110). Such a marinade is made as follows:

¼ pint oil; 4 oz. each minced carrot and onion; 1 oz. minced shallots; ½ garlic clove, crushed; ½ oz. parsley stalks; 1 sprig each rosemary and thyme; 1 bayleaf; ½ pint vinegar; 1 bottle white wine; 1 oz. salt; ¼ oz. peppercorns; 2 oz. brown sugar.

Heat the oil in a saucepan, add the minced carrot and onion and fry them, stirring frequently. When they begin to brown, add the shallots, garlic and bouquet of herbs. Moisten with the vinegar, white wine and a quart and a half of water. Cook for twenty minutes, then add the salt, peppercorns and brown sugar. Cook on for another ten minutes, then pass through a sieve.

If this marinade is to be used for soaking the meat, it must be allowed to get quite cold before being poured around and over it.

MIREPOIX

Here and there throughout the recipes for sauces in this book the word mirepoix is used. This preliminary operation is carried out as follows:

2 medium-sized carrots; 2 sticks heart of celery; 1 tbs. raw lean ham or gammon of bacon; 1 sprig thyme; ½ bayleaf; butter; 2 tbs. Madeira.

Cut into fine dice the red part only of the carrots, the onions and the celery. Add the ham or gammon of bacon, also cut into fine dice, a sprig of thyme, and half a bayleaf, crushed. (Fresh or slightly salted breast of pork may be used instead of the ham.) Stew all these together in a little butter and swill the pan with the Madeira. For Fast Days the mirepoix can be made *maigre* by omitting the meat.

GRAVY (from Roasts)

Gravy is correctly made by adding water or other liquid to the juices which drop from the joint during its cooking. Neither it nor the roasting dish should be burned, but it should remain ready to be scraped from the bottom of the dish when it has been loosened by the moistening agent. The quantity required should in the end be reduced by a third for the sake of its flavour, and then passed through a fine cloth. It should neither be clarified nor have all the fat removed, as this contributes notably to the taste. For joints roasted in the oven, it is as well to see that the baking-dish is chosen to fit the size of the joint, so that the danger of burning during the cooking is lessened.

CARAMEL (for Sauces, Soups and Stews)

Put one pound of castor or moist sugar and a good tablespoonful out of three quarters of a pint of water into a heavy enamelled saucepan, and stir it over the heat until it becomes dark brown. Then add the rest of the water, stir it until it boils and simmer until it reaches the thickness of syrup, which should take about three quarters of an hour. Be careful that the sugar does not burn, or the caramel will taste bitter. When cold, bottle it.

MUSHROOM COOKING LIQUOR

Choose mushrooms all much the same size, peel them and remove the stalks; for every half-pound put them into a mixture of six table-spoonfuls of water, a heaped saltspoon of salt, and the juice of half a lemon, which has previously been brought to the boil. Add also an ounce of butter and boil quickly for four or five minutes. The mushrooms are now done and if wished can be kept in an earthenware terrine with their liquid, covered with buttered paper or foil.

INFUSION

A preparation made by pouring water, cold or boiling, over vegetable substances so as to their flavour, e.g. making tea. The length of time is dictated by the requirements of the recipe in question.

Savoury Sauces

AGRO-DOLCE SAUCE I

2 tsp. castor sugar; 2 tbs. vinegar; ½ pint brown stock (p. 32); 1 tbs. almonds; 2 tbs. sultanas.

Put the castor sugar into a saucepan and stir it over the heat until it browns, then add the vinegar and cook together for a couple of minutes. Now add the stock and simmer for twenty minutes longer. Finish by adding a tablespoonful of blanched and chopped almonds and two tablespoonfuls of sultanas, and serve as hot as possible.

Use with meat or poultry, particularly duck.

AGRO-DOLCE SAUCE 2

2 tbs. castor sugar; 1 clove garlic; 1 bayleaf; ¼ pint wine vinegar; 2 tbs. grated bitter chocolate.

Put the sugar into a saucepan with a peeled clove of garlic and a bay-leaf, and cook slowly until the sugar goes slightly yellow. Then stir in the wine vinegar and grated chocolate, mix well together and simmer for a few minutes. Strain this into the sauce from the braised meat (see below), mix well together, and pour over the meat on serving.

Use with braised meats.

AGRO-DOLCE SAUCE 3

2 tbs. brown sugar; 2 tbs. currants; 4 oz. grated chocolate; 1 tbs. candied orange peel; 1 tbs. candied lemon peel; 1 tbs. capers; 6 fl. oz. vinegar; pine-kernels or blanched almonds.

Mix well together the brown sugar, currants, grated chocolate, chopped candied orange and lemon peel, the capers, and the vinegar, and leave for two hours. Then simmer for ten minutes. A table-

38

spoonful of pine-kernels or a dozen blanched almonds, finely chopped, can be added if liked.

Use with hare or venison.

AIOLI I

Garlic; salt; egg yolk; ¼ pint olive oil; lemon juice.

This is made in the same way as Mayonnaise (p. 28), but first of all two cloves of garlic for each person are pounded in a mortar to a fine paste. A little salt is then added and an egg yolk for every two persons. Mix together, and add the olive oil drop by drop, stirring all the time, and finish the sauce with a dash of lemon juice. For each additional egg yolk use almost another quarter of a pint olive oil. The aïoli should be practically solid.

Use with boiled fish or chicken, snails, boiled potatoes, French beans and hard-boiled eggs.

AIOLI 2 (without eggs)

5–6 cloves garlic; panada or floury potato; salt and pepper; olive oil.

A Provençal recipe reads as follows: Skin five or six cloves of garlic; pound them in a mortar with a little panada or even a floury potato, which must however be quite cold. Season with salt and pepper, and when you have a smooth purée, gradually add enough olive oil, stirring all the time, until you have a thick Mayonnaise.

Use with salads and as for Mayonnaise.

ALEXANDRA SAUCE

Add half a teacupful of cooked asparagus cut in small pieces to half a pint of White Sauce (p. 24).

Use with boiled chicken.

ALMOND SAUCE I

1 dessertsp. vinegar; 1 oz. breadcrumbs; 2 oz. ground almonds; 2 tsp. chopped parsley; 1 tsp. grated onion; juice of 1 lemon; salad oil.

Pour the vinegar over the breadcrumbs, and mix this with the ground almonds, chopped parsley and grated onion. Pound well together and add the lemon juice and enough salad oil to make the sauce the consistency of Bread Sauce. Serve as it is for cold fish, but if the fish is hot, the sauce must be heated.

Use with fish.

ALMOND SAUCE 2

½ *oz. ground sweet almonds; 1 oz. blanched pistachio nuts; 1 tbs. cold White Sauce (p. 24); 3 egg yolks; ½ tsp. salt; ¼ tsp. pepper; juice of 1 lemon; parsley; chives; chervil; tarragon.*

Pound smoothly the ground sweet almonds and blanched pistachio nuts. Add to them the cold White Sauce, and rub through a sieve. Now add the beaten egg yolks, salt and pepper. Beat well, and then gradually mix in the olive oil, as for Mayonnaise, with the lemon juice. When the sauce is smooth, add one and a half tablespoonfuls of the mixed herbs, all blanched for three minutes and then passed through a fine sieve.

Use with cold fish.

ALMOND SAUCE 3

2 *oz. blanched almonds; ½ oz. butter; 1 heaped dessertsp. flour; ¼ pint stock; salt; mace; sugar; 1 tbs. cream.*

Mince finely the blanched almonds, and brown them in the butter, stirring them all the time so that they colour evenly. Now add the flour, cook a little, and moisten with the stock made with the giblets of the bird. Season with a pinch of salt, mace and sugar. Just before serving, add the cream.

Use with turkey or fowl.

ALMOND SAUCE 4 (Swiss)

3 *oz. almonds; 1 tbs. butter; 1 tbs. flour; ½ pint stock or stock and milk; salt; lemon juice; lump of sugar.*

Blanch the almonds and grind them coarsely. Fry them golden brown in the butter, and stir in the flour. Moisten with the stock or stock and milk mixed, and simmer for ten minutes, stirring. Finish with salt, lemon juice and a lump of sugar.

Use with boiled turkey.

ALSATIAN SAUCE

¼ pint port wine; nutmeg; salt and pepper; red-currant jelly; 3 tbs. grated horseradish; 3 tbs. cream.

Put the port wine into a small saucepan with a pinch of nutmeg and a seasoning of salt and pepper. Let this boil down by a third, and then add twice the quantity of melted red-currant jelly, the grated horse-radish and a little cream. Cook on for a minute or two, stirring, but without boiling, and serve.

Use with hare or venison.

ANCHOVY BUTTER SAUCE

Put into a saucepan eight tablespoonfuls of Half-Glaze Sauce (p. 26) and when boiling, add one ounce of Anchovy Butter (p. 181). Stir continuously until the butter is melted and serve.

See also Sauce au Beurre d'Anchois (p. 118).

Use with fish.

ANCHOVY SAUCE 1 (Sauce Anchois)

2 oz. butter; 1 oz. flour; ¾ pint fresh single cream; salt and pepper; 2 oz. Anchovy Butter (p. 181) or 2 tsp. anchovy essence.

Make a white roux (p. 23) with the butter and flour, moisten with the cream, season with salt and pepper, and bring to the boil. Finish at the last moment with the Anchovy Butter or anchovy essence.

Use with fish.

ANCHOVY SAUCE 2 (Sauce Anchois)

To three quarters of a pint of White Wine Sauce (p. 179) add two and a half ounces of Anchovy Butter (p. 181) and the fillets of three salted anchovies cut in small dice.

Use with fish.

ANCHOVY SAUCE 3

3 salted anchovies; flour; butter; ½ pint stock; nutmeg; pepper; gherkins; capers.

Soak the salted anchovies in cold water for an hour, then chop them up, sprinkle them with a little flour and fry them in butter. Add the stock to moisten, with nutmeg, pepper and a few gherkins cut in dice. Simmer gently, and at the last finish with a few capers.

Use with beef.

ANCHOVY SAUCE 4 (American)

2 tsp. anchovy paste; 6 fl. oz. Melted-Butter Sauce (p. 96); 2 fl. oz. sherry.

Dissolve the anchovy paste in the Melted-Butter Sauce, then gradually stir in the sherry, and heat to boiling point. Simmer for about five minutes, stirring hard all the time, until the sauce thickens slightly. (In America, this sauce, generally used with fish, also accompanies veal or pork chops and boiled or roast chicken.)

Use with fish, veal, pork chops or boiled or roast chicken.

ANCHOVY SAUCE 5 (Austrian)

3 salted anchovies; ½ onion; parsley; 2 tbs. flour; 1 oz. lard.

Leave the salted anchovies to soak all night, then clean them and chop them finely with half an onion and a little parsley. Brown the flour in the lard, add the anchovy mixture, cook together for a minute or two and then moisten with water. Cook for another quarter of an hour, and the sauce is ready.

Use with fish.

ANISETTE SAUCE (Sauce à l'Anisette)

1 quart shrimps; oil; vinegar; mustard; 1 handful mixed parsley, chives, chervil and tarragon; lemon juice; 1–2 tbs. anisette.

Shell the shrimps and pound them. Make a sauce with these and enough oil and vinegar to give a sauce-like consistency, adding mustard, chopped herbs, salt, pepper, a squeeze of lemon juice and a small glass of anisette.

Use with cold lobster.

APPLE SAUCE I

1 lb. cooking apples; butter; sugar.

'Pare, core and slice your apples, put them in a saucepan, with as much water as will keep them from burning, set them over a very slow fire, keep them close-covered till they are all of a pulp, then put in a lump of butter, and sugar to your taste, beat them well, and send them to the table in a china bason.' (Mrs Raffald, 1769.)

Use with goose.

APPLE SAUCE 2

1 slice bread; vinegar; 3 cooking apples; 6 burnt almonds; 1 chopped onion; rind of an orange; pepper; mixed spice; white wine.

Dip a slice of well-toasted bread in vinegar and put it into a saucepan with the peeled and cored apples cut in slices, the almonds, the onion, the red outside rind of an orange, pepper and mixed spice to taste and equal quantities of wine and vinegar to moisten. Boil all together until the apples are quite soft, then pass through a sieve and serve very hot.

Use with roast mutton.

APPLE AND HORSERADISH SAUCE I (Austrian)

1 lb. cooking apples; 2 tbs. sugar; 1-2 tbs. grated horseradish or horseradish sauce.

Cook the apples in their skins until they are soft, then pass them through a sieve. While still hot, mix in the sugar, heat up again and then add one or two tablespoonfuls, to taste, of grated horseradish or bottled horseradish sauce. Serve cold.

Use with veal or pork.

APPLE AND HORSERADISH SAUCE 2 (Austrian)

2 tbs. vinegar; 2 tsp. sugar; salt; 1 lb. cooking apples; 1–2 tbs. grated horseradish or bottled horseradish sauce.

Make a mixture of the vinegar, sugar and a pinch of salt. Now peel and grate the apples, occasionally moistening them with a little of the vinegar mixture to prevent them from discolouring. When all is mixed together, add one or two tablespoonfuls, to taste, of grated horseradish or bottled horseradish sauce, and leave covered for an hour before serving.

Use as above.

APPLE AND HORSERADISH SAUCE 3

1 lb. cooking apples; 2 tbs. grated horseradish; 2 hard-boiled eggs; capers; salt and pepper; Mayonnaise (p. 28).

Make a purée of apples as in Apple and Horseradish Sauce 1 and mix it with the grated horseradish and sieved hard-boiled egg yolks. Chop the capers and egg whites finely and add, season with salt and pepper, and mix with a Mayonnaise Sauce.

Use as above.

ASPARAGUS SAUCE

25 asparagus tips; butter; ½ pint White Sauce (p. 24); salt and pepper; ½ tsp. lemon juice.

The boiled or tinned asparagus tips are lightly fried in a little butter, then simmered for a quarter of an hour in the White Sauce, seasoned with salt and pepper and tinted with a little greening, if desired. The sauce is then passed through a fine sieve, reheated and finished with the lemon juice.

Serve with asparagus.

ASPARAGUS MAYONNAISE SAUCE

Make a thick and dryish purée of green asparagus tips, and when it is cold, mix it with an ordinary Mayonnaise Sauce (p. 28).

Serve with asparagus.

AVGOLEMONO SAUCE (Greek)

1 oz. butter; 2 level tbs. flour; ½ pint stock; 2 eggs; juice of 1–2 lemons.

Make a blond roux (p. 24) with the butter and flour, and let it cook for a few minutes. Then add hot stock by very slow degrees, so as to keep the sauce nice and smooth. When cooked keep it hot while you beat the eggs until light and frothy, and to these add, beating all the time, first the lemon juice and then two tablespoonfuls of cold water. Now add the sauce to this, a large spoonful at a time, and return all to the pan, being careful, however, that it is not allowed to boil or it will curdle.

Use with fish, meat or chicken.

BACON SAUCE

¼ lb. streaky bacon; 1 small onion; 1 scant tbs. flour; pepper; 2 tbs. vinegar.

The bacon is diced and fried lightly with a small finely chopped onion and the flour is sprinkled in and browned slightly, seasoned with pepper. Add half a pint of water and the vinegar and simmer for a few minutes.

Use with roast chicken or veal.

BAGNA CAUDA

6 oz. butter; 4 oz. oil; 4 cloves garlic; 6 anchovies; salt; 1 truffle.

This interesting hot sauce from Piedmont is described thus by the late Countess Morphy in her *Good Food from Italy*:
'Put six ounces of butter in a saucepan with four ounces of oil and four very finely chopped cloves of garlic, and stir over a slow heat until very hot, but without allowing the garlic to brown. It should remain quite white. Then add six well-washed and boned salted anchovies, finely chopped, and stir the mixture over a slow heat, adding a good pinch of salt. In Piedmont where truffles are abundant, one white thinly sliced truffle is added. The sauce is used for cooked vegetables, such as cardoons, celery, pimientos, etc., and is served in a characteristic way. The saucepan in which it is made is put in the middle of the table, over a spirit lamp, so that it is kept very hot, and

each person dips their piece of cardoon or stick of celery or slice of pimiento in the hot and tasty sauce. For special occasions there are also small individual pans, each with its own lamp, which are given to each guest.'

Use with cooked vegetables.

BALBIRNIE SAUCE

Mix thoroughly a small shallot chopped as fine as possible, one mustardspoonful of mustard, and one tablespoonful of oil, then add a little salt, one tablespoonful of vinegar and two of ketchup.

Use with cold pheasant.

BARBECUE SAUCE I (American)

¼ *lb. butter; ½ pint vinegar; ½ tsp. mustard flour; 1 tbs. chopped onion; 2 tbs. Worcestershire sauce; 1 tbs. chilli sauce; ¼ lemon; 1 tsp. brown sugar; ½ red chilli pepper.*

Put into a saucepan the butter, vinegar, mustard flour, chopped onion, Worcestershire sauce, chilli sauce, the juice of quarter of a lemon and two slices of lemon, the brown sugar, and half a red chilli pepper ground up. Let the butter melt on a low heat and then keep the sauce warm. The sauce is used to baste barbecued roast meat while it is cooking, the basting being done every ten minutes.

Use for basting grilled or roast joints.

BARBECUE SAUCE 2

Mix together six teaspoonfuls of melted butter, a dessertspoonful of vinegar, half a teacupful of red-currant jelly, a quarter of a level teaspoonful of dry mustard, and salt and cayenne pepper to taste.

Use for heating up slices of cold lamb, beef or mutton.

BASIL SAUCE

1 handful fresh basil; ½ oz. butter; ½ pint gravy or stock; flour; 1 egg yolk.

Stew the finely chopped basil in the butter, then moisten it with the gravy or stock after adding a little flour, and season and simmer for twenty minutes. At the last moment before serving, whip in the egg yolk.

Use with roast wood pigeon.

BÉCHAMEL SAUCE
Basic sauce (p. 24).

BÉCHAMEL MAYONNAISE SAUCE (American)
Add half a pint of Mayonnaise Sauce (p. 28) to half a pint of hot Béchamel Sauce (p. 24) and serve at once.

Use with fish.

BEER SAUCE (Swiss)
1 pint lager beer; 1 tsp. vinegar; 1 tsp. brown sugar; 2 tbs. chopped onion; 1 clove garlic; 1 bayleaf; 1 tsp. butter; salt and pepper; cinnamon; 2 tbs. potato flour.

Put the beer into a saucepan with the vinegar, brown sugar, finely chopped onion, the clove of garlic, the bayleaf, butter, and a seasoning of salt, pepper and cinnamon. Simmer for fifteen minutes and then strain. Now mix the potato flour with a little cold water, add this to the sauce, and cook until it thickens.

Use with baked fish.

BEETROOT SAUCE
1 small onion; 1 clove garlic; 1½ oz. butter; 1 scant tbs. flour; 3 fl. oz. red wine vinegar; 2 tsp. tarragon vinegar; salt and pepper; ½ small beetroot; cream.

Fry the finely chopped onion and clove of garlic in the butter until they are browning, then add the flour and brown that as well. Now moisten with the red wine vinegar, and if you like, the tarragon vinegar, seasoning with salt and pepper. When the sauce has thickened, strain it, and add the beetroot which has been boiled, peeled and then rubbed through a wire sieve. Stir all together over the fire until quite smooth and either serve it as it is or finish it with a little cream.

Use with sea bream and other similar fish.

BLOATER SAUCE (Swiss)

1 bloater; 3 tbs. butter; 4 tbs. flour; 1 onion; ½ pint milk or fish stock (p. 34).

Pour hot water over the bloater, leave it for four minutes, then skin and bone it and pound the flesh finely. Make a White Sauce (p. 24) with the butter, flour, finely chopped onion and milk or fish stock. Add the pounded bloater, cook for half an hour, rub through a sieve and reheat.

Use with boiled fish.

BOURGEOISE SAUCE (Sauce à la Bourgeoise)

Blanch a tablespoonful of mixed chopped parsley, chervil and tarragon, drain them and mix them with half a pint of brown stock and a little warm meat glaze (p. 33), a little mustard, castor sugar, pepper and lemon juice.

Excellent with fresh boiled beef.

BRAIN SAUCE

Chopped onion is lightly browned in butter, flour is added and then a moistening of the liquor from a cooked sheep's head, flavoured with a little vinegar. The coarsely chopped brains are added at the last moment.

Use with sheep's head.

BREAD SAUCE I

½ pint milk; 1 very small onion; 1 clove; 2 oz. breadcrumbs; salt and pepper; ¼ oz. butter; 1 tbs. cream.

Put the milk into a saucepan with the onion stuck with a clove, and bring to the boil. Add the breadcrumbs and simmer gently for twenty minutes. Then remove the onion, add salt and pepper to taste, stir in the butter and cream, and serve.

Use with roast chicken, roast lamb or pheasant.

BREAD SAUCE 2

In some parts of England, Bread Sauce is flavoured lightly either with saffron powder or with saffron shreds first infused in a little of the milk.

Use as above.

BREAD SAUCE 3

2 oz. fine breadcrumbs; 1 shallot; ½ pint milk; ¼ oz. butter; cayenne; salt; cream.

Put the breadcrumbs, the peeled shallot, milk, butter, cayenne pepper and salt to taste into a saucepan, and boil them together for five minutes, stirring all the time. Then take out the shallot, and finish with a spoonful of cream.

Use as above.

BREAD SAUCE 4 (American)

1 pint milk; 4 oz. white breadcrumbs; 1 onion; 6 cloves; 1 level tsp. salt; cayenne; butter; 2 oz. coarse crumbs.

Cook the milk in a double saucepan for half an hour, with the white crumbs and the onion stuck with the cloves. Take out the onion, and add to the thickened breadcrumbs the salt, a little cayenne pepper, and two level tablespoonfuls of butter. Finally, sprinkle with the coarse crumbs browned in a little butter.

Use as above.

BROWN SAUCE I
Basic sauce (see p. 26).

BROWN SAUCE 2

6 button mushrooms; 1 small onion; 1 small carrot; 2 oz. butter; 1½ oz. flour; 1 pint brown stock (p. 32) 1 tomato.

Slice the mushrooms, the onion and the carrot, and fry them brown in the butter. Sprinkle with the flour, brown this too, then add the stock and a sliced tomato.

Bring to the boil and simmer for ten minutes or so, then season to taste, strain, reheat and serve.

Use with casserole of beef or lamb.

BROWN SAUCE 3 (Brown Gravy) (American)

½ *slice onion; 1 oz. butter or bacon fat; 2 tbs. flour; 8 fl. oz. brown stock (p. 32) or water; salt and pepper.*

Lightly brown the onion in the butter or bacon fat, then take out the onion and stir on until the butter gets well browned. Now add the flour, and brown that too, moistening with the stock or water and seasoning with salt and pepper. Bring to the boil, and boil for two minutes.

Use with roast joints.

BROWN ALMOND SAUCE

4 oz. almonds; 1 oz. butter; 1 oz. flour; salt and pepper; 1 pint single cream.

Blanch and chop the almonds, brown them in the butter, then add the flour with salt and pepper, and moisten slowly with the cream. Bring to boiling point and serve.

Use with roast chicken or veal.

BROWN MUSHROOM SAUCE 1

Add six ounces of sliced fried mushrooms to half a pint of any Brown Sauce. Tinned mushrooms can be used, in which case, add also a little of the liquid from the tin.

Use with beef or lamb.

BROWN MUSHROOM SAUCE 2

2 level tbs. butter; onion juice; 3 level tbs. flour; 8 fl. oz. single cream; ½ lb. mushrooms; salt; paprika pepper; 1 level tsp. beef extract.

Brown the butter slightly, then add a few drops of onion juice and the flour, and brown that too. Moisten gradually with the cream, and then add the sliced fried mushrooms. Season with salt and paprika pepper, add the beef extract at the last, and it is ready.

Use as above.

BROWN WINE SAUCE (German)

1 carrot; 1 onion; 1 oz. butter; 1½ oz. flour; 1 pint well-flavoured stock; salt and pepper; 1½ tbs. white wine.

Slice the carrot and onion and brown them well in the butter. Add the flour, brown this too, and then moisten with the stock. Simmer for ten minutes, then season with salt and pepper. After straining it finely, add the white wine and heat up again.

Use with beef or lamb.

BUTTER SAUCE

1 oz. flour; 3½ oz. butter; 3 egg yolks; ⅛ pint cream; ¼ lemon.

Mix the flour with an ounce of melted butter and dilute with a pint of boiling salted water. Stir briskly to ensure a perfect liaison, and do not allow to boil. Add immediately the egg yolks mixed with the cream and the lemon juice. Rub through a fine sieve, and finish with two and a half ounces of fresh butter. Be careful that the sauce does not boil after it has been thickened.

Use with fish, eggs, chicken, vegetables.

CAMBRIDGE SAUCE

6 eggs; 4 anchovies; 1 tsp. capers; 2–3 tsp. mixed chervil, tarragon and chives; 1 tbs. mustard; ⅕ pint oil; 1 tbs. vinegar; cayenne; 1 tsp. chopped parsley.

Pound together the yolks of the hard-boiled eggs, the washed and dried fillets of anchovies, the capers, and the chopped chervil, tarragon and chives. When the whole forms a fine paste, add the mustard, oil and vinegar, and proceed as for a Mayonnaise. Season with a little cayenne, rub through a fine sieve into a bowl, applying pressure with a spoon. Stir with a whisk to smooth it, and finish with the parsley.

Use as for Mayonnaise.

CAPER SAUCE 1 (White)

½ *pint White Sauce (p. 24); salt and pepper; 2 tsp. pickled capers.*

Make half a pint of White Sauce, using half milk and half liquor in which the fish or meat has been boiled. Season with salt and pepper, and finish with the pickled capers, whole or cut in halves. The sauce should not boil after the capers have been added. Some like to add a little of the caper liquor as well.

Use with boiled fish or meat.

CAPER SAUCE 2 (Brown)

Brown Sauce (p. 26); 3 tbs. capers; parsley; 2 lemons; shallot.

Put into a saucepan three soup-ladlefuls of Brown Sauce, the capers, some finely minced parsley, the juice of two lemons and a little minced shallot. Cook all together, bringing to the boil, for twenty minutes or so, and serve with pike, barbel and other freshwater fish that need a somewhat piquant sauce.

Use with freshwater fish.

CAPER SAUCE 3 (for Salmon)

butter; 1 tbs. flour; 2 tsp. lobster spawn; ½ pint strongly flavoured white stock (p. 33); essence of anchovies or shrimps; capers.

Put a small piece of butter into a saucepan and when it is melted, stir in the flour. Add the pounded lobster spawn and stock, and boil all together until it is the colour of Lobster Sauce. Add a little essence of anchovies or of shrimps, and at the last, some chopped capers.

Use with salmon or sea-trout.

Savoury Sauces

CAPER SAUCE 4 (American)

1 level tsp. dry mustard; 1 level tsp. sugar; 1 level tsp. salt; 2 egg yolks; 2 tbs. lemon juice; 6 fl. oz. salad oil; 1 tsp. onion juice; 1 small red pepper; 1 tbs. chopped capers; 1 tbs. chopped pickled cucumber.

Beat the dry mustard, sugar and salt with the egg yolks, then add lemon juice, and beat again. Now add the salad oil by degrees, as in making a Mayonnaise Sauce, and when it is ready, add to it the onion juice, the red pepper minced, and the chopped capers and chopped pickled cucumber.

Use as for Mayonnaise.

CAPER SAUCE 5 (Italian)

Mince an anchovy and let it melt in a little oil and butter over a gentle heat. Add four ounces of capers, three tablespoonfuls of vinegar and some chopped parsley. Serve hot or cold.

Use with fish.

CAPER SAUCE 6 (Italian)

Mix four ounces of capers well with the juice of a lemon and a quarter of a pint of olive oil.

Use with fish.

CAPER SAUCE 7 (Scandinavian)

1 tbs. butter or margarine; 2 tbs. flour; ¾ pint fish stock (p. 34); 2 tbs. chopped capers; 1 tbs. cream or 1 egg yolk.

Make a White Sauce (p. 24) with the butter or margarine, flour and well-flavoured fish stock. To this add the chopped capers and a little of the caper liquid, and cook on for ten minutes. Bind at the last with the cream or egg yolk.

Use with fish.

CARROT SAUCE

1 large carrot; 1 oz. butter; ¾ pint stock; salt and pepper; 1 tsp. lemon juice; 1 tsp. finely chopped parsley.

Cook the grated carrot in the butter for ten minutes, then add the stock, season with salt and pepper and simmer for half an hour. Strain, add the lemon juice and parsley, bring to the boil, and it is ready.

Use with boiled meat.

CASANOVA MAYONNAISE SAUCE

6 eggs; ½ pint olive oil; 1 tsp. tarragon vinegar; 4 truffles or mushrooms; shallot.

Make a Mayonnaise Sauce (p. 28) with three egg yolks, the olive oil and tarragon vinegar, and add to it the finely shredded truffles or mushrooms, a pinch of minced shallot, the finely shredded whites of three hard-boiled eggs and their sieved yolks.

Use as for Mayonnaise.

CAULIFLOWER SAUCE (American)

White Sauce (p. 24); ½ pint chicken stock (p. 33); 4–5 tbs. cauliflower.

Make a White Sauce with three level tablespoonfuls of butter, five tablespoonfuls flour, salt, pepper, and one and half pints of milk, and add to it the chicken stock and cooked cauliflower flowerets.

Use with boiled chicken.

CELERY SAUCE

¾ pint white stock (p. 33); mace; 2 sticks celery; 1½ oz. butter; 1½ oz. flour; ½ pint milk; 2 tbs. cream.

Put the stock into a pan with a blade of mace and the white part of two sticks of celery previously blanched. Simmer until the celery is tender, then rub through a sieve. Melt the butter, stir in the flour, cook gently for five minutes, then add the milk and celery purée. Bring to the boil, correct the seasoning, and finish with the cream.

Use with boiled chicken.

CHAMPAGNE SAUCE

1 large wineglass champagne; 2 cloves; 6 peppercorns; 1 bayleaf; 1 tsp. sugar; 8 fl. oz. Espagnole Sauce (p. 26); mushroom cooking liquor (p. 37).

Put the champagne into a saucepan with the cloves, peppercorns, bayleaf and sugar. Let them infuse for five minutes over the heat, then add the Espagnole Sauce and, if possible, a little mushroom cooking liquor. Simmer together for ten minutes and then strain.

Use with ham.

CHAUDFROID SAUCE 1 (White) (Escoffier)

1 pint Velouté Sauce (p. 24); ¾ pint white poultry jelly; ½ pint very fresh cream.

Boil the Velouté Sauce and add the poultry jelly. Put the pan on a medium heat, reduce the sauce by a third, stirring constantly the while, and gradually add the cream. When the sauce has reached the desired consistency rub it through a fine sieve and stir it frequently while it cools for fear of a skin forming on its surface, for if this happened it would have to be strained again. When dishing up, the sauce should be cold, so that it may properly coat immersed solids and yet be liquid enough to permit the latter to be easily steeped in it.

Use to coat cold chicken, or fish, or cold moulded mousses.

CHAUDFROID SAUCE 2 (Ordinary)

Make as above, using Allemande Sauce (p. 25) instead of Velouté, and using only a quarter of a pint of cream.

Use as above.

CHAUDFROID SAUCE 3 (Brown) (Escoffier)

1 pint Half-Glaze Sauce (p. 26); 2 fl. oz. truffle essence; ¾ pint white poultry jelly; Madeira or port.

Put the Half-Glaze Sauce into a sauté-pan with the truffle essence. Put the pan on the heat and reduce its contents, and at the same time add the poultry jelly in small quantities at a time. The degree of reduction of this sauce is a good third, but to be quite certain, a test of its consistency may be made by cooling it a little. After the reduction, carefully taste, and rectify the seasoning if necessary; mix a little Madeira or port with the sauce, away from the heat, and strain through muslin. Stir the sauce now and then while it cools until it is sufficiently liquid, and at the same time consistent enough, to coat immersed solids evenly with a film of sauce.

Use as above.

CHAUDFROID SAUCE À L'AURORE (Pink)

White Chaudfroid Sauce may be coloured by the addition of a fine red tomato purée or, if a pale pink is desired, by an infusion of paprika.

Use as above.

CHAUDFROID SAUCE AU VERT-PRÉ (Green)

When making a white Chaudfroid Sauce, add to the Velouté (p. 24) at the same time as the jelly an infusion prepared as follows: boil a quarter of a pint of white wine, and add to it a pinch of chervil stalks, a similar quantity of tarragon leaves, chives and parsley leaves. Cover, allow infusion to proceed away from the heat for ten minutes, and strain through linen. Lastly colour the sauce a pale green.

Use as above.

HEESE SAUCE I

White Sauce (p. 24); cheese.

This is an ordinary White Sauce to which grated cheese is added at the last minute, and stirred until it melts. The usual proportions are a tablespoonful of cheese to three quarters of a pint of sauce, but more may be added according to taste. Some like to add a touch of made mustard as well, and a dash of cayenne pepper.

Use with fish, eggs, meat and vegetables.

CHEESE SAUCE 2 (American)

To half a pint of White Sauce (p. 24), add two tablespoonfuls grated cheese, half a teaspoonful of Worcestershire sauce, and some paprika pepper. When the cheese has quite dissolved, stir together and serve. *See also* Sauce Mornay (p. 140).

Use as above.

CHERVIL SAUCE

Season half a pint of fresh double cream with salt and pepper and mix in a handful of finely cut fresh chervil.

Use with roast chicken.

CHESTNUT SAUCE 1

2 doz. chestnuts; ½ pint brown gravy (p. 36); sherry.

Boil the chestnuts until they are soft, remove the skins and rub them through a sieve. Add them to the gravy, heat through without boiling, and just before the sauce comes to the table, add a sherryglass of sherry.

Use with chicken.

CHESTNUT SAUCE 2

20 chestnuts; butter; salt and pepper; glaze (p. 33); mushrooms or truffles; consommé.

Boil the shelled chestnuts until they are tender, then remove the inside skin and rub them through a sieve. Put them into a stewpan with a small pat of butter, a little salt and pepper, a little glaze, some mushrooms or mushroom peeling or truffles chopped fine to flavour, and a ladleful of consommé. Stir until hot, and serve.

Use with turkey or fowl.

CHESTNUT SAUCE 3

1 onion; 3 tbs. butter; 3 tbs. flour; ½ pint stock; 1 bayleaf; sage; thyme; 6 peppercorns; salt; 12 sieved boiled chestnuts; 3 fl. oz. port.

Fry the chopped onion golden-brown in two tablespoonfuls of the butter, add the flour and brown that too. Then add the stock, bayleaf, a small pinch each of powdered sage and thyme, the peppercorns, and a seasoning of salt. Simmer, covered, for twenty minutes. Then strain and add the chestnuts, one tablespoonful of butter, and the port.

Use with venison or hare.

CHILLI SAUCE 1

¾ pint vinegar; 6 tomatoes; 4 green sweet peppers; 1 onion; 1 tbs. sugar.

Boil the vinegar and add to it the chopped tomatoes, chopped peppers, minced onion and a scant tablespoonful of sugar. Boil all together for an hour, then strain and season to taste.

Use with any fish or meat.

CHILLI SAUCE 2

2 red chillies; 1 tbs. capers; parsley; 3 fl. oz. sherry; juice of ½ lemon.

Chop up the red chillies with the capers and a little parsley. Season with salt and sugar, and moisten with the sherry and lemon juice. Mix all well together.

Use with fish or meat e.g. grilled.

CHIVES SAUCE 1

Pass the yolks of three hard-boiled eggs through a fine sieve and mix them with three tablespoonfuls of salad oil, a teaspoonful of vinegar, two tablespoonfuls of finely chopped chives, and a seasoning of salt and pepper.

Generally served with fish.

CHIVES SAUCE 2

1 oz. butter; 2 tbs. chopped chives; 1 tbs. flour; 1 tbs. vinegar; 3 tbs. cream; salt and pepper.

Fry the chopped chives and flour in the butter until the flour is a light brown. Then add a little water, the vinegar, cream, and a seasoning of salt and pepper. Stir until the sauce is thick, and serve hot.

Use with boiled meat.

CHIVES SAUCE 3 (Swiss)

1 oz. butter; 1 oz. flour; ¼ pint cream; 1 pint veal stock (p. 32); 2 tbs. chopped chives.

Make a white roux (p. 23) with the butter and flour, and moisten with the cream. Bring the stock to the boil and add it gradually to the thickened cream, also adding chopped chives. Simmer for a quarter of an hour in a double saucepan, but do not allow the sauce to boil.

Use with fish or boiled meat.

CHIVES MAYONNAISE SAUCE

To an ordinary Mayonnaise Sauce (p. 28) add as much chopped chives as your taste directs.

Particularly good with cold salmon or lobster.

CHRISTOPHER NORTH'S SAUCE

1 dessertsp. castor sugar; salt; cayenne; 2 tbs. Harvey's sauce; 1 dessertsp. mushroom ketchup; 1 tbs. lemon juice; 1 large glass port wine.

Put into a jar or basin the castor sugar, a saltspoonful of salt, and a good saltspoonful of cayenne pepper. Mix well together and add by degrees the Harvey's sauce, mushroom ketchup, lemon juice and port wine. Put the receptacle into a pan of boiling water and let the contents heat until nearly boiling, but not quite.

Use with roast duck, goose or pork.

CIDER SAUCE

½ pint cider; ¾ pint Brown Sauce (p. 26); salt and pepper; 1 bayleaf; 2 cloves.

Mix the cider with the Brown Sauce and season with salt, pepper, the bayleaf and cloves. Stir well together and simmer quietly until the sauce reaches the desired consistency. Then strain and serve.

Use with meat.

COCKLE SAUCE (Portuguese)

2 oz. butter; 2 oz. flour; 1 pint fish stock (p. 34); cockles; salt and pepper; lemon juice.

Make a smooth sauce with the butter, flour and fish stock, or fish stock and milk, and when it is finished, garnish it with cooked shelled cockles and season it with salt, pepper and a little lemon juice. Simmer together gently for about a quarter of an hour and serve.

Use with boiled fish.

COLONY CLUB SAUCE (American)

Mix together a bottle of A1 sauce, half a teaspoonful of dry mustard, one tablespoonful of Worcestershire sauce, and half a pint of double cream.

Use with ham, tongue or fillet of beef.

CRAB SAUCE I

1 crab; 1 pint Melted-Butter Sauce (p. 96); Fish Velouté (p. 24) or Béchamel Sauce (p. 24); cayenne; lemon.

Put the flaked meat and soft parts of a cooked crab into the pint of sauce, and heat it through without letting it boil. At the last minute, add a touch of cayenne pepper and a squeeze of lemon.

Use with boiled fish.

CRAB SAUCE 2

½ pint White Sauce (p. 24); crab; 1 tsp. anchovy essence; lemon juice; cayenne.

Make half a pint of White Sauce with stock made by simmering the cleaned and broken crab-shell in milk and water, and when it is ready, add one teacup of cut-up crab-meat with the anchovy essence, a few drops of lemon juice, and a touch of cayenne pepper.

Use with boiled fish.

CRAB-MEAT SAUCE (American)

½ *pint White Sauce (p. 24) or Cream Sauce (p. 62); 3 oz. crab-meat; 1 tsp. Worcestershire sauce or sherry.*

To the White Sauce or Cream Sauce add the flaked, cooked or tinned crab-meat, and either the Worcestershire sauce or the sherry, according to taste. Increase the seasoning of the sauce a little.

Use with boiled fish.

CRANBERRY SAUCE I

1 lb. cranberries; ¾ lb. sugar.

Put the cranberries into a deep saucepan with the sugar and a pint of water. Bring to the boil, put on the lid and cook slowly for about ten minutes or until the skins break. Then skim the sauce, and let it get cold.

Use with turkey.

CRANBERRY SAUCE 2 (Hungarian)

Cook half a pound of cranberries for a few minutes with a very little water, a small glass of sweet white wine, and the grated rind and juice of half a lemon and of one orange, with sugar and spice to taste.

Use with duck and game.

CRANBERRY AND APPLE SAUCE

1 lb. cranberries; 1 lb. diced apple; 6 oz. sugar

Put the cranberries and diced apple into a saucepan with three quarters of a pint of water, stew them until soft and then rub them through a sieve. Add six ounces of sugar (or more, to taste) and reheat.

Use with roast fowl.

CRANBERRY AND CELERY SAUCE

Shred two inside sticks of fresh celery and add to half a pint of hot cranberry jelly. Stir until it begins to set.

Use with chicken or turkey.

CRAPAUDINE SAUCE

To half a pint of hot light Piquante Sauce (p. 145) add four chopped mushrooms and a teaspoonful of dry mustard mixed smoothly with two teaspoonfuls of tarragon vinegar. Boil for five minutes before serving.

Use with grilled poultry or meat.

CREAM SAUCE 1 (American)

An ordinary White Sauce (p. 24), in which cream is substituted for the usual milk, becomes a Cream Sauce.
See also Sauce Crème (p. 128).

Use with fish, eggs, poultry, meat and vegetables.

CREAM SAUCE 2 (German)

Thicken the drained drippings left in the pan from roasting game with flour, let it brown a little, and then moisten with cream, fresh or sour. When thick and smooth, season with salt and pepper. If sour cream is used, add a touch of lemon juice at the last.

Use with game.

CREAMY EGG SAUCE (American)

Pound four hard-boiled egg yolks to a paste with a quarter of a tea-spoonful each of salt and paprika pepper. Then gradually work in four tablespoonfuls of creamed butter, three dessertspoonfuls of double cream, and two tablespoonfuls of lemon juice.

Use with hot asparagus or cauliflower.

CRÉOLE SAUCE I

3 dessertsp. chopped onion; 6 dessertsp. chopped green pepper; 2 tbs. butter; 3–4 tomatoes; 2 oz. mushrooms; stuffed olives; ½ pint Brown Sauce (p. 26).

Fry the chopped onion and finely chopped green pepper in the butter for five minutes. Then add the fresh, stewed or tinned tomatoes, the peeled and sliced mushrooms, and a few sliced stuffed olives, and cook for two minutes only. Add a scant half pint of Brown Sauce, bring to the boil, and it is ready to serve.

Use with meat and poultry.

CRÉOLE SAUCE 2

onion; green sweet peppers; butter; flour; stock; tomato juice; salt and pepper; nutmeg; horseradish; cream.

Chop up equal amounts of onion and green sweet peppers, and half-cook them in butter. Sprinkle with flour and moisten with stock, adding tomato juice, a good deal of salt and pepper, a little nutmeg and some horseradish pounded smooth with a little cream. Cook until the sauce is thick and smooth, and serve.

Use as above.

CRUMB SAUCE (American)

Mix together a teacupful of melted butter, four tablespoonfuls of dry breadcrumbs and a teaspoonful of minced chives. Toss until browned.

Use with asparagus, baked onions or cauliflower.

CUCUMBER SAUCE I

¼ pint double cream; 3 dessertsp. vinegar; salt and pepper; 1 cucumber.

Whisk the cream until it is thick but not stiff, then add the vinegar gradually, beating all the time. Season with a quarter of a teaspoonful of salt and a very little pepper, and lastly fold in the peeled, chopped and well-drained cucumber.

Use with fish.

CUCUMBER SAUCE 2 (Créole)

Peel and grate a cucumber and add to it three dessertspoonfuls of made mustard, mixing well together. Then add the juice of a lemon and the well-beaten yolk of an egg.

Use as above.

CUCUMBER SAUCE 3

1 cucumber; 1 oz. butter; ½ pint Béchamel Sauce (p. 24); lemon juice; salt and pepper; green colouring.

Stew the peeled and thickly sliced cucumber, less the seeds, in the butter for about half an hour, then add the Béchamel Sauce, a little lemon juice, salt and pepper to taste, and a touch of green colouring. Cook for two or three minutes longer, then pass through a sieve.

Use with fish, veal or poultry.

CUCUMBER SAUCE 4 (Hungarian)

Mix an ounce of flour smoothly with two or three tablespoonfuls of sour cream, and then add light stock until the right creamy thickness is obtained. Cut half a small peeled pickled cucumber into very thin strips, add them to the sauce and bring it to the boil.

Use with fish.

CUCUMBER SAUCE 5 (Russian)

2 medium-sized salted cucumbers; 1 pint stock; brown roux (p. 25); mushroom cooking liquor (p. 37).

Peel the salted cucumbers and chop them up. Put the peel into a pint of good stock, bring it to the boil and simmer for three quarters of an hour. Strain and thicken with brown roux. Bring to the boil again, add some mushroom cooking liquor, and just before serving, stir in the chopped cucumber flesh.

Use with fish.

CUCUMBER HOLLANDAISE SAUCE I

This is a Hollandaise Sauce (p. 27) flavoured with chilli vinegar, to

Savoury Sauces

which, after it is made, a pared, chopped and well-drained cucumber is added. It is best to squeeze the cucumber as dry as possible in butter muslin before putting it in the sauce.

Use with fish, e.g. salmon.

CUCUMBER HOLLANDAISE SAUCE 2 (American)

Make a Hollandaise Sauce (p. 27), and when it is ready add a little salt, a suspicion of cayenne pepper, and half a chopped and drained peeled cucumber, which has been well squeezed in a cloth to rid it of as much moisture as possible.

Use with fish.

CUCUMBER MAYONNAISE SAUCE

Add half a peeled, chopped or diced cucumber, which has been well drained, to an ordinary Mayonnaise Sauce (p. 28). A little chopped parsley or chervil may also be added.

Use with fish.

CUMBERLAND SAUCE I

½ tsp. finely chopped shallots; ½ orange; ¼ lemon; 2 tbs. red-currant jelly; ¼ pint port wine; ½ tsp. mustard; cayenne pepper and powdered ginger.

Blanch the shallots then press them dry. Grate half a teaspoonful each of fine julienne strips of orange and lemon rind; scald them for two minutes, then drain them and allow to cool. Dissolve the red-currant jelly, add the port wine, the shallots, orange and lemon rind, the juice of the orange and the lemon, the mustard and a little cayenne pepper and powdered ginger. Mix well together.

Use with cold venison.

CUMBERLAND SAUCE 2 (German)

2 tbs. red-currant jelly; 1 mustardspoon dry mustard; red wine.

Put the red-currant jelly into a bowl and stir and mash it with a wooden spoon until there are no lumps left. Now stir in smoothly the dry mustard, and lastly add enough red wine to make the sauce as thick as cream.

Use with ham and gammon.

CURRANT SAUCE 1

1 oz. dried currants; 1 oz. breadcrumbs; 1–2 cloves; nutmeg; butter; sugar; 1 wineglass sweet white wine.

This is a traditional English sauce to accompany sucking-pig. Boil half a pint of water for a minute or two, then add the currants, breadcrumbs, cloves, a touch of grated nutmeg, a small piece of butter, sugar to taste and the sweet white wine. Simmer all together for a few minutes, and serve in a sauceboat.

Use with sucking-pig.

CURRANT SAUCE 2 (Scandinavian)

3 tbs. washed dried currants; 1 tbs. margarine or butter; 2 tbs. flour; 1 tbs. black treacle; 1 tbs. vinegar; salt and pepper.

Boil the currants in three breakfastcupfuls of water until they are tender, and stir this into a white roux (p. 23) made with the margarine or butter and flour, adding the treacle. Boil this mixture for ten minutes, and then add the vinegar and salt and pepper to taste.

Use with fish.

CURRANT JELLY SAUCE

Pass half a pint of Brown Sauce (p. 26) through a strainer, add four ounces of warm red-currant jelly, and stir until the jelly has quite melted. Heat up and serve.

Use with mutton and lamb.

CURRY SAUCE 1

1 oz. butter; 6 oz. minced onions; ½ oz. parsley stalks; 2 oz. minced celery; thyme; bayleaf; mace; ½ tsp. curry powder; 1 oz. flour; ¾ pint white stock (p. 33).

Slightly brown in butter the minced onions, parsley stalks, minced celery, a very small sprig of thyme, a little bit of bayleaf and a little mace. Sprinkle with the flour and curry powder. Cook the flour a little and then moisten with the stock. Boil gently for three quarters of an hour and then sieve.

Use with anything suitable for a curry.

CURRY SAUCE 2

2 small onions; 2 oz. butter; 1 clove chopped garlic; 1 tbs. curry powder; salt; ½ lb. tomatoes; lemon.

Fry the onions finely sliced in the butter, adding the garlic. Stir in the curry powder, and season with salt. Now add the peeled and quartered tomatoes and a little water, enough to make a thickish sauce. Simmer until the tomatoes are a mash. Add a touch of lemon at the last.

Use as above.

CURRY SAUCE 3 (American)

Season Onion Sauce (p. 103) with curry powder.

Use as above.

CUSTARD SAUCE

3 egg yolks; 2 tbs. cream; 2 oz. fresh butter; 1 tsp. sugar; salt; juice of 1 lemon or tarragon vinegar with chilli vinegar.

Put the egg yolks in a saucepan resting over hot water, and gradually mix in the cream and butter. Stir until it thickens, adding the sugar, a pinch of salt, and at the last the juice of a lemon or a small teaspoonful of tarragon vinegar with a few drops of chilli vinegar. Strain into a warmed sauce-boat and serve.

Use with salmon.

DEVIL SAUCE I

1½ oz. butter; 3 oz. shallots; 2 green chillies; 1 tsp. green ginger; ½ pint stock; ¼ pint claret; 1 tbs. chilli vinegar; 1 tbs. chutney; 1 tsp. sugar or red-currant jelly.

Melt the butter in a saucepan and fry in it lightly the finely minced shallots with the minced green chillies and a teaspoonful of scraped green ginger. When the shallot is slightly browned, moisten with the stock, claret and chilli vinegar. While this is heating up, stir in the chutney and the sugar or red-currant jelly. Bring to the boil, skim and simmer for a quarter of an hour. Then strain and when cold skim again if necessary.

Used with grilled fish or meat.

DEVIL SAUCE 2

2 finely chopped shallots or 1 small onion; ½ oz. butter; 1 tbs. mixed mustard; 1 dessertsp. Worcestershire sauce; cayenne; salt; ½ pint Half-Glaze Sauce (p. 26); parsley.

Fry the shallots or a small onion in the butter until they are golden, then add the mustard, Worcestershire sauce, a seasoning of cayenne pepper, a touch of salt and the Half-Glaze Sauce. Bring to the boil, skim and strain, and finish with a little chopped parsley.

Use as above.

DEVILLED SAUCE

2 oz. sliced shallots; ⅓ pint white wine; ½ pint Half-Glaze Sauce (p. 26); cayenne.

Put in a saucepan the sliced shallots and white wine. Reduce the latter to two thirds, add the Half-Glaze Sauce, reduce again to two thirds, season strongly with cayenne pepper, and strain through muslin.

Use with grilled fowl and pigeon.

DILL SAUCE I (Czechoslovakian)

1 handful dill; 1 oz. fat; 3 tbs. flour; 1 lump sugar; 1 tbs. vinegar; 1 tbs. cream.

Stew the finely chopped dill in the fat, add the flour, cook for a minute or two, then moisten with a teacupful of water, off the heat. When the sauce is thick, add gradually a pint of hot water, the sugar and vinegar. Cook for five or six minutes, and at the end stir in the cream.

Use with fish.

DILL SAUCE 2 (Scandinavian)

1 tbs. fat; 2 tbs. flour; 1 pint meat stock (p. 32) or fish stock (p. 34); 2 tbs. chopped dill; salt and pepper; vinegar; 1 egg yolk.

Make a white roux (p. 23) with the fat and flour, moisten with the meat stock (or fish stock, if the sauce is for fish), and cook for ten minutes. Then add the dill and season with salt, pepper and a dash of vinegar. Bind at the last with an egg yolk.

Use with meat or fish.

DILL SAUCE 3 (Swiss)

1 oz. butter; 1 oz. flour; ¼ pint cream; 1 pint veal stock (p. 32); 2 tbs. chopped dill.

Make a white roux (p. 23) with the butter and flour and moisten smoothly with the cream. Bring the stock to the boil and add it gradually to the thickened cream, adding the chopped dill. Simmer for a quarter of an hour in a double saucepan, but do not let the sauce boil.

Use with boiled meat.

DRAWN BUTTER SAUCE

See Melted-Butter Sauce (p. 96) and add a touch of lemon juice.

Use with anything suitable for a white sauce.

DUTCH SAUCE I

1 egg white; pepper and salt; 2 tsp. minced parsley; 1 small minced shallot; 1 tsp. mustard; 2 tbs. olive oil; 2 tsp. tarragon vinegar; horseradish.

Beat up the egg white with a little white pepper and salt, the parsley, shallot, mustard and olive oil. Whisk it well together, and add about a dessertspoonful of tarragon vinegar. Grated horseradish may be added, if liked.

Use with pike, cod or baked fresh haddock.

DUTCH SAUCE 2 (Brown)

2 oz. butter; 1 tbs. flour; 1 onion; glaze; ½ pint brown stock (p. 32); 1 sprig parsley; 1 sprig watercress; celery; just under 1 oz. lean bacon; 1 wineglass sherry; salt and pepper; sugar.

Make a brown roux (p. 25) with the butter and flour, and in another pan brown the sliced onion, adding it to the roux when ready. Now melt a piece of glaze the size of an egg in the stock, to make a good thick sauce. Add this to the roux and flavour with the parsley, watercress, a little celery, the bacon and sherry. Season to taste with salt and pepper, add a small pinch of sugar, and boil all together for a short while. Then strain through a sieve or tammy-cloth.

Use with pike or cod or stuffed baked haddock.

DUTCH SAUCE 3 (White)

2 oz. butter; 1 tbs. flour; 6 fl. oz. milk; 2 egg yolks; ½ lemon; salt and pepper; 1 tbs. cream.

First melt the butter and mix in the flour. Add the milk smoothly, bring to boil, and boil for ten minutes. Mix the egg yolks with the juice of the lemon-half, season with salt and pepper and keep ready in a pan for the bain-marie. Add the sauce to this, mix all well, and heat through in the bain-marie, making sure that it does not boil. Just before sending to table, add a tablespoonful of cream.

Use with anything suitable for a white sauce.

EAST INDIA MAYONNAISE SAUCE

Chop and rub a clove of garlic through a fine sieve, mix it with a teaspoonful of good curry powder, and add it to a thick Mayonnaise Sauce (p. 28).

Use with fish cakes or cold boiled salmon.

EEL SAUCE (English)

½ lb. skinned eels; 1 oz. lean ham; ¾ pint stock; 1 small sliced onion; 1 carrot; 1 bayleaf; 6 peppercorns; salt and pepper.

Wash the skinned eels, cut into short lengths, and put these with the chopped ham into a saucepan with the stock, onion, a few thin slices of carrot, bayleaf and peppercorns. Season with salt and pepper and simmer gently for half an hour. Then strain and use.

Use with boiled eel.

EGG SAUCE I

Add a chopped hard-boiled egg or two to half a pint of White Sauce (p. 24). Some like to add a little chopped parsley.

Use with boiled fish.

EGG SAUCE 2 (American)

5 hard-boiled eggs; 8 fl. oz. stock; 1 tsp. Worcestershire sauce; salt and pepper; 2 tsp. flour; 2 tbs. cream; 1 tsp. chopped parsley; 2 tsp. lemon juice.

Dice the hard-boiled eggs and put them into a saucepan with the hot stock, Worcestershire sauce and salt and pepper to taste. Simmer for five minutes and then add the flour which has been first mixed smoothly with the cream and chopped parsley. Bring to the boil and add the lemon juice off the fire.

Use with roast chicken or a suitable vegetable.

EPICUREAN SAUCE I

½ cucumber; ¼ pint Mayonnaise Sauce (p. 28); ⅛ pint cream; 1 tsp. anchovy essence; 1 dessertsp. chutney and pickled gherkins; 1 tbs. tarragon vinegar; ⅛ pint aspic jelly; salt; pepper; castor sugar.

Peel and cut the cucumber into small pieces, cook these till tender in salted water, drain the pieces and rub them through a fine sieve. Mix the Mayonnaise Sauce with the cream, anchovy essence and chutney and pickled gherkins. Mix the cucumber purée with the tarragon vinegar and nearly cold aspic jelly, then blend this mixture with the first one, seasoning with salt, pepper and a little castor sugar.

Use as for Mayonnaise.

EPICUREAN SAUCE 2

½ *pint double cream; 2 tbs. Mayonnaise (p. 28); 1½ tbs. grated horseradish;*
½ *level tsp. made mustard; salt; cayenne'*

Beat the cream stiffly and fold into it the Mayonnaise, grated horse-radish, mustard, half a level teaspoonful of salt and a little cayenne pepper.

Use as above.

ESPAGNOLE SAUCE

Basic sauce (see p. 26).

FENNEL SAUCE I

This is simply White Sauce (p. 24) to which a handful of chopped fennel has been added in the same way as parsley for Parsley Sauce. The sauce should not be allowed to boil after the fennel has been added and if its rather definite flavour is found to be too strong, the fennel may first be blanched. Sometimes fennel and parsley are added together in equal quantities. This old-fashioned sauce was popular with boiled salmon and boiled mackerel, Gooseberry Sauce (p. 78) being handed with the latter as well.

Use with boiled salmon and boiled mackerel.

FENNEL SAUCE 2 (Swedish)

1 tbs. butter; 2 tbs. flour; 1 scant pint stock; 1½ tbs. white vinegar; 2 tsp. sugar; 2 tbs. chopped fennel; 1 egg yolk.

Make a White Sauce (p. 24) with the butter, flour and stock. Cook for ten minutes or so, then add the white vinegar, sugar and chopped fennel, which may first be blanched, if preferred. Bind at the last with an egg yolk.

Use with boiled mutton, a sprig of fennel having also been boiled with the meat.

FIGARO SAUCE (American)

Add to a Henriette Sauce (p. 83) three teaspoonfuls of Worcestershire sauce.

Use with baked or boiled fish.

FINISTE SAUCE (American)

2 level tbs. butter; ½ level tsp. made mustard; 1 tsp. lemon juice; 1½ tsp. Worcestershire sauce; ¾ lb. stewed and sieved tomatoes; cayenne.

Brown the butter, and then add the mustard, lemon juice, Worcestershire sauce, tomatoes and a little cayenne pepper as a finishing touch.

Use with grilled fish or meat.

FISH SAUCE 1

Flavour quarter of a pint of whipped double cream to taste with a teaspoonful of Harvey's sauce, Worcestershire sauce, anchovy essence and a seasoning of pepper. Serve very cold or slightly iced.

Use with almost any fish dish.

FISH SAUCE 2

1 fresh egg; 2 tbs. olive oil; 1 dessertsp. chilli vinegar or 1 tbs. tarragon vinegar; salt; ⅛ pint double cream; cress.

Break the egg into a basin and, stirring with a wooden spoon, add gradually the olive oil, and chilli vinegar or tarragon vinegar. Add salt, the whipped cream and a tablespoonful of the tiny leaves of cress (the kind sold with mustard) but use the small cress only.

Use as above.

FISH SAUCE 3

1 sprig each of thyme and winter savory; 2 sprays parsley (without stalks); 3 anchovies; 2 tbs. sherry; 1 tbs. lemon juice; 1 small piece lemon peel; 1 small onion; 1 blade mace; 2 cloves; 6 white peppercorns; ¼ lb. clarified butter; 1 tsp. flour; ¼ pint double cream.

Put into a mortar the thyme, winter savory and parsley, and pound these up with the anchovies, sherry, lemon juice, onion, lemon peel, mace, cloves and peppercorns. Then strain through a tammy-cloth, add the clarified butter, the flour and the double cream. Then boil all together stirring all the time.

Use as above.

FISH SAUCE 4 (American)

4 egg yolks; 2 tbs. olive oil; 2 tsp. vinegar; ¼ tsp. dry mustard; 1 onion; 1 tsp. chopped parsley; 2 tsp. capers; 3 small vinegar pickles.

Beat the egg yolks well and add very gradually a tablespoonful of olive oil. Then add a teaspoonful of vinegar, another tablespoonful of oil and another teaspoonful of vinegar. Now add the dry mustard and salt and pepper. Mix well again and finally add the finely chopped raw onion, chopped parsley, capers and the vinegar pickles cut in tiny pieces. The sauce should be well peppered.

Use as above.

FISH SAUCE 5 (Greek)

1 tbs. flour; fat; 2–3 cloves garlic; salt and pepper; 2 fl. oz. vinegar; rosemary.

Mix the flour with the fat left in the pan after frying fish, adding the cloves of garlic, salt, pepper, vinegar, four fl. ounces of hot water and a leaf of rosemary. Stir and boil until thick, and then strain. (If you wish to have a very strong garlic flavour, add the garlic chopped; otherwise leave it whole.)

Use with fried fish.

FLUFFY CUCUMBER SAUCE (American)

Peel, chop and drain well a medium-sized cucumber. Whip stiffly a quarter of a pint of double cream, fresh or sour, and fold in the cucumber with a little salt and three teaspoonfuls of vinegar.

Use with cold fish or meat.

FLUFFY MUSTARD SAUCE (American)

2 oz. brown sugar; 1½ tbs. dry mustard; 3 eggs; 4 fl. oz. vinegar; 4 fl. oz. stock; salt and pepper.

Separate the eggs. Mix together the brown sugar with the dry mustard and the beaten egg yolks in a double saucepan. Add the vinegar and stock, and heat well through, stirring all the time. Add a seasoning of salt and pepper, fold in the stiffly beaten egg whites, and continue cooking for about five minutes longer.

Use with fish, beef or ham.

FRIED BREAD SAUCE

4–5 shallots; 1 tbs. diced ham; ½ pint consommé (stock); 2 oz. breadcrumbs; butter; parsley; lemon juice.

Chop the shallots and cut the ham into tiny dice, and simmer them in consommé for ten minutes. Bind with breadcrumbs fried in butter, and finish with chopped parsley and a squeeze of lemon juice.

Use with roast meats.

FRONTIER SAUCE (American)

1½ tbs. butter; 2 tbs. flour; salt and pepper; Tabasco sauce; ½ pint tomato juice; 2 tbs. mushroom liquor; 2 tbs. cream.

Make a white roux (p. 23) with the butter and flour, add salt, pepper, a dash of Tabasco sauce, the tomato juice and mushroom liquor. Cook for five minutes, stirring all the time, and when the sauce is thick and smooth, add the thick cream.

Use with macaroni or spaghetti.

GAME SAUCE

game; 1 small onion; ½ small carrot; ¼ small turnip; 1 glass sherry; bouquet of parsley, thyme and bayleaf; mace; 1 clove; salt and pepper; 1 pint Espagnole Sauce (p. 26).

Chop up the bones and trimmings of game into small pieces, slice thinly the onion, carrot and turnip, and put these into a saucepan with the sherry, the bouquet of herbs, a blade of mace, a clove and salt and pepper. Simmer for five minutes, then add the Espagnole Sauce, bring to the boil, skim and cook gently for a quarter of an hour. Then pass through a sieve or tammy and reheat to serve.

Use with roast game, e.g. pheasant.

GARLIC SAUCE I

Peel thirty blanched almonds, and pound them to a paste. Mix with a quarter of a pint of olive oil, adding finely chopped garlic to taste.

Use with fish or salads.

GARLIC SAUCE 2 (Italian)

garlic; breadcrumbs; salt; wine vinegar.

For each person allow two cloves of garlic, not quite a level table-spoonful of breadcrumbs, a good pinch of salt and enough wine vinegar to moisten to the consistency of very thick cream. The garlic is pounded with the breadcrumbs and a little salt, and the vinegar is stirred in gradually until the right thickness is reached.

Use with fried salt cod, calf's liver.

GARLIC AND TOMATO SAUCE (Italian)

2–3 cloves garlic; 2–3 tbs. olive oil; 1 lb. ripe tomatoes; salt and pepper; chopped marjoram and parsley.

Slightly colour the sliced cloves of garlic in the olive oil, then add the chopped tomatoes and simmer for an hour or so, seasoning with salt, pepper and a little chopped marjoram and parsley. When the sauce is reduced to a purée, it is ready.

Use with fish, meat or pasta.

GENOVESE SAUCE I (Italian)

1 clove garlic; 3–4 sprigs parsley; $\frac{1}{2}$ oz. capers; 1 salted anchovy; 3 stoned olives; yolk of 1 hard-boiled egg; bread; vinegar; $\frac{1}{4}$ pint olive oil; salt and pepper.

Chop the garlic and parsley and pound them in a mortar with the capers, anchovy, olives, the egg yolk and a heaped tablespoonful of bread previously soaked in vinegar. When they are a smooth paste, add the olive oil gradually, and finally a tablespoonful of vinegar. Then season with a little salt and pepper.

Use with boiled fish or pasta.

GENOVESE SAUCE 2 (Italian)

3 cloves garlic; handful sweet basil leaves; salt; 2 handfuls grated Parmesan cheese, 4 tbs. olive oil.

This is the *Pesto alla Genovese*, enough for two people. Chop the garlic very finely with the sweet basil leaves. Put into a mortar, add a pinch of salt and pound with the grated Parmesan cheese, adding the olive oil very gradually and stirring with a wooden spoon, as in making Mayonnaise Sauce. Finally, dilute with three or four tablespoonfuls of boiling water.

Use as above.

GERMAN SAUCE

3 medium-sized potatoes; yolks of 3 hard-boiled eggs; 2 tbs. olive oil; 1 tbs. vinegar; parsley.

Boil the potatoes in salted water, skin them and let them cool and then pass them through a potato-ricer or sieve. Add the egg yolks and mix well together, moistening with the olive oil and vinegar. Pass all through a hair-sieve, and add a little finely minced parsley. The sauce should be pretty thick, but if it seems too thick, dilute with a little more vinegar.

Use with boiled beef.

GHERKIN SAUCE 1

1 small onion; 1 medium-sized carrot; 1 tomato; 1 oz. dripping; 1 oz. flour; 2 tsp. mushroom ketchup; 1 tsp. vinegar; ¾ pint stock; 1 tbs. chopped gherkins.

Peel and chop the onion, slice up the carrot and tomato. Make a roux with the dripping and flour, add the onion and carrot and cook over a low heat until they are lightly browned. Then add the tomato, the mushroom ketchup, vinegar and stock, and simmer for twenty minutes after bringing to the boil. Strain and season to taste, and finally stir in the chopped gherkins.

Use with grilled steak or chops.

GHERKIN SAUCE 2

½ pint wine vinegar; 1 sprig thyme; 1 bayleaf; 1 clove garlic; 2 finely chopped shallots; salt and pepper; cayenne; ½ pint stock; parsley; 3–4 tbs. minced pickled gherkins.

Boil gently for about half an hour the wine vinegar, thyme, bayleaf, garlic, shallots, salt, pepper and a little cayenne pepper. Then add the stock, which can be thickened or not as you wish, mix well together, bring to the boil and add at the last some finely chopped parsley and the peeled and minced pickled gherkins.

Use with boiled beef or lamb.

GHERKIN SAUCE 3 (Russian)

Boil up one or two large pickled gherkins, peeled and sliced, in a couple of tablespoonfuls of their pickling liquid, and thicken with a small nut of butter kneaded with a tablespoonful of flour. Thin down with a little water, if the sauce gets too thick.

Use with boiled fish.

GLOUCESTER SAUCE

Mayonnaise Sauce (p. 28) made with sour cream and finished with a few drops of Escoffier sauce and chopped fennel.

Use as for Mayonnaise.

GOLDEN MALAGA SAUCE (American)

Bind half a pint of White Sauce (p. 24) with an egg yolk, and add a teacupful of peeled white grapes, with their seeds removed, cut in quarters.

Use with grilled fish or boiled white fish.

GOOSEBERRY SAUCE 1 (Swiss)

3 tbs. butter; 4 tbs. flour; 1 pint milk; ½ lb. green gooseberries; 1 tsp. chopped onion; salt and pepper; 1 tsp. sugar.

Make a White Sauce (p. 24) with the butter, flour and milk. Meanwhile stew the gooseberries with the chopped onion in a little water until they are soft enough to pass through a sieve. Mix the gooseberry purée with the White Sauce, and season with salt, pepper and a teaspoonful of sugar. Serve hot.

Use with mackerel.

GOOSEBERRY SAUCE 2

Half a pint of scalded gooseberries are mixed with a pint of Drawn Butter Sauce (p. 69).

Use with lamb.

GOOSEBERRY SAUCE 3

Cook together gently a pint of green gooseberries, half a pint of water, half an ounce of butter, and two or more ounces of sugar to taste. Then sieve, re-heat and serve.

Use with goose or duck.

GOOSEBERRY SAUCE 4

1 pint Melted-Butter Sauce (p. 96); 1 lb. green gooseberries; ½ pint white wine; 3 oz. sugar.

Have ready the Melted-Butter Sauce. Boil the green gooseberries in boiling water for five minutes, then drain them and put them into a saucepan with the white wine and sugar. Cook them gently, rub them through a sieve, and add this purée to the Melted-Butter Sauce.

Used with grilled or poached fillets of mackerel.

GOOSEBERRY SAUCE 5 (Hungarian)

1 lb. green gooseberries; 1–2 egg yolks; 1 oz. flour; ¼ pint sour cream; about ¼ pint stock or water; salt or sugar; lemon juice.

Gently stew the gooseberries in a little water until they are soft but not mashed. Beat together the egg yolks, flour and sour cream, and mix this with the gooseberries, being careful to keep them whole. Add stock or water with salt or sugar according to taste, and bring gently to the boil. A finishing touch of lemon juice may be added.

Use with boiled meat.

GRAPEFRUIT SAUCE

2 tbs. butter; 2 oz. toasted breadcrumbs; salt and pepper; 3 tbs. Tomato Sauce (p. 170); ½ pint grapefruit juice; 1 egg; 2 tbs. sharp fruit jelly.

Melt the butter and stir in the toasted breadcrumbs, salt, pepper and Tomato Sauce. Then stir in gradually the grapefruit juice and beaten egg. Stand on the stove and simmer until all is well blended, and just before serving stir in two tablespoonfuls of quince, red-currant or any sharp fruit jelly.

Use with game, mutton or beef.

GRAPE JUICE SAUCE

3 level tsp. cornflour; 6 fl. oz. grape juice; lemon juice.

Mix the cornflour with three tablespoonfuls of cold water, then add quarter of a pint of hot water. Cook until the sauce thickens, then add the grape juice and the juice of a lemon. Serve hot.

Use with ham.

GRATIN SAUCE

5–6 button mushrooms; 1 glass sherry; ½ oz. meat glaze (p. 33); 1 tbs. finely chopped parsley; 2 shallots or 1 very small onion; ½ pint Espagnole Sauce (p. 26); anchovy essence.

Simmer the button mushrooms, cut up small, with the sherry, meat glaze, finely chopped parsley and shallots or onion, until the liquid is well reduced. Then add the Espagnole Sauce and anchovy essence, cook together for five minutes and it is ready.

Use with beef or lamb.

GREEN SAUCE I

1 handful parsley and chervil; spinach and tarragon leaves; 2 chopped gherkins; 2 tbs. capers; butter; Béchamel Sauce (p. 24).

Scald the parsley and chervil in boiling water with a few spinach and tarragon leaves, plunge them into cold water, dry them and pound them in a mortar, adding the chopped gherkins, capers and a piece of butter. Pass through a sieve, and use this butter to finish a Béchamel Sauce.

Use with boiled fish or poultry.

GREEN SAUCE 2 (Spanish)

olive oil; 2–3 cloves garlic; flour; 2 pints stock; 1 tbs. chopped parsley; salt and pepper; 1 handful cooked green peas; 1 handful green asparagus tips.

Heat a little olive oil in a saucepan and add the garlic, chopped. When this begins to brown, stir in a little flour and add gradually the hot stock and chopped parsley. Season with a little salt and pepper, and cook until it is reduced by half. Now add the green peas and asparagus tips, and simmer for ten minutes longer.

Use with lamb or roast chicken.

GREEN PEA SAUCE (American)

To half a pint of White Sauce (p. 24) add a tablespoonful of chopped sweet red pepper and five tablespoonfuls of cooked or drained tinned peas.

Use with fish or omelette.

GREEN PEA MAYONNAISE SAUCE

Cook and sieve enough green peas to a thinnish purée to fill one breakfastcup, and use this when cold to mix with an ordinary Mayonnaise Sauce (p. 28).

Use with potato salad.

GREEN RANCHERO SAUCE (Mexican)

4 green tomatoes; 2 medium-sized onions; 3 red chilli peppers; 3 tbs. parsley; salt.

Chop together for ten minutes the green tomatoes, onions and red chilli peppers, seeds and all. Pour over them half a pint of boiling water, bring to the boil, and boil for twenty minutes. Rub through a

sieve, and add the chopped parsley, and enough salt to give a high
seasoning. Serve hot.

Use with veal or beef.

GUAYMAS SAUCE

Have ready a quarter of a pint of cold Tomato Sauce (p. 170) and just
before serving, add to it just over twice as much Mayonnaise Sauce
(p. 28) and two tablespoonfuls of finely shredded olives.

Use as for Mayonnaise.

GUBBINS SAUCE

*butter; 2 tsp. made mustard; 1 dessertsp. vinegar; ½ dessertsp. tarragon
vinegar; ½ tbs. cream; salt; black pepper; cayenne.*

Here are Nathaniel Gubbins' own instructions: 'The legs and wings
of fowl, turkey, pheasant, partridge or moor-hen should only be
used. Have these scored across with a sharp knife, and divided at the
joints. And when your grill is taken, "hot as hot", but not *burnt*, from
the fire, have poured over it the following sauce. Be very particular
that your cook pours it over the grill just before it is served up. And
it is of the most vital importance that the sauce should be made, and
well mixed, on a plate *over hot water* – for instance, a slop-basin should
be filled with boiling water and a plate placed atop.

Melt on the plate a lump of butter the size of a large walnut. Stir
into it, when melted, two teaspoonfuls of made mustard, then a
dessertspoonful of vinegar, half that quantity of tarragon vinegar, and
half a tablespoonful of cream – Devonshire or English. Season with
salt, black pepper and cayenne, according to the (presumed) tastes and
requirements of the breakfasters.' (*Cakes and Ale* by Edward Spencer
(Nathaniel Gubbins), 1900.)

Use with grills.

HAM SAUCE

*½ pint Espagnole Sauce (p. 26) or Brown Sauce (p. 26); 2 tbs. finely shredded
cooked ham; 2 tsp. finely chopped parsley; salt and pepper; 1 tsp. lemon
juice.*

To the hot Espagnole Sauce or Brown Sauce, add the ham, parsley, salt and pepper, and lemon juice. The ham is added first and simmered with the sauce for five minutes or so, and the rest of the ingredients are added off the heat afterwards.

Use with duck and game.

HANOVERIAN SAUCE

1 Seville orange; 1 tbs. castor sugar; juice of 1 lemon; ½ tbs. mustard; 2 tbs. oil; 2 tbs. port wine.

This is noted in a Victorian cookery book as excellent for boar's head etc. Mix the outer rind of a Seville orange cut in very thin small slices with the castor sugar; squeeze the juice of a lemon over the two together and add the mustard, oil and port wine.

Use with wild duck.

HENRIETTE SAUCE (American)

Flavour a Hollandaise Sauce (p. 27) made with two eggs with one or two tablespoonfuls of tomato purée and a scant dessertspoonful of chopped parsley.

Use with fish or grilled cutlets.

HERB SAUCE (German)

2 oz. butter or lard; 2 oz. flour; 1 pint half cream half milk; parsley; thyme; dill; chives; 1 hard-boiled egg; salt; mustard.

Make a white roux (p. 23) with the butter or lard and flour, and moisten it with the cream milk. Chop up finely as many mixed fresh herbs as you can, for example, parsley, thyme, dill, chives and so on, as well as a hard-boiled egg. Add these to the sauce, and season with salt and a little mustard to taste.

Use with fish or poultry.

HERRING SAUCE (Russian)

2–3 salted herrings; 1 onion; butter; flour; 1 pint stock; lemon juice; 2 tbs. sour cream.

Bone, skin and fillet the salted herrings, and finely chop the flesh together with an onion. Fry both these in a little butter, sprinkle with flour, and moisten with the boiling stock. Simmer for half an hour, then strain and add a little lemon juice and the sour cream.

Use with boiled fish.

HOLLANDAISE SAUCE 1
Basic sauce (see p. 27).

HOLLANDAISE SAUCE 2 (Cold)
3 egg yolks; ½ pint milk; salt and pepper; ¼ pint wine vinegar; 1 tsp. chopped onion.

Make a custard with the egg yolks and milk, seasoning it with salt and pepper. Now boil the vinegar with a little salt and the chopped onion until there is only a good tablespoonful left, then strain this and let it get cold. Then stir it very gradually into the cold custard.

Hollandaise Sauce Variations

Cucumber Hollandaise Sauce 1, 2	Sauce Foyot
Custard Sauce	Sauce Maltaise
Dutch Sauce 3	Sauce Marguéry
Figaro Sauce	Sauce Mousseline
Henriette Sauce	Sauce Noisette
Horseradish Hollandaise Sauce	Sauce Paloise
Lobster Hollandaise Sauce	Sauce Valois
Mock Hollandaise Sauce	Shrimp Sauce 1
Sauce Béarnaise	Toulouse Sauce

HORSERADISH SAUCE 1
1 small horseradish root; ½ pint Béchamel Sauce (p. 24); 1 egg yolk; 3 tbs. sour cream; tarragon or chilli vinegar.

Scrape the horseradish root into the Béchamel Sauce, simmer this for half an hour, then sieve and reheat, binding with an egg yolk beaten into the sour cream with a few drops of tarragon or chilli vinegar.

Use with fish or boiled beef.

HORSERADISH SAUCE 2

2 tbs. grated horseradish; 1 tbs. white vinegar; ¼ pint double cream; 1 tsp. sugar.

Soak the grated horseradish in the white vinegar for a quarter of an hour. Then stir it, drained, into the double cream with the sugar just before serving. Some prefer to whip the cream slightly, but not too much.

Use with boiled beef.

HORSERADISH SAUCE 3

Tie four tablespoonfuls of roughly scraped horseradish in a cloth and boil it with a piece of salt beef. When the beef is done, mix the horseradish with a mixture of enough beer and vinegar to make a sauce, and serve it with the meat.

Use with salt beef.

HORSERADISH SAUCE 4

½ tsp. made mustard; ½ tsp. castor sugar; ½ tsp. tarragon vinegar; 2 tbs. finely grated horseradish; ¼ pint double cream.

Mix together, in this order, the made mustard, the castor sugar, the tarragon vinegar, the finely grated horseradish, and the slightly whipped cream. The cream should be mixed in very lightly, and the sauce stood on ice until it is wanted.

Use with roast chicken or game and for hot or cold salmon.

HORSERADISH SAUCE 5 (Hungarian)

Mix some grated horseradish with orange juice and a little water, adding sugar to taste.

Use with fish or boiled beef.

HORSERADISH SAUCE 6 (Swiss)

2 horseradish roots; ½ pint milk; 2 lumps sugar; 1 tsp. ground almonds; 2 tbs. vinegar.

Grate the horseradish and mix this with the cold milk. Add the sugar, the ground almonds and the vinegar, and warm gently. It is then ready. If this is to be served cold, let it wait an hour before serving.

Use with fish or boiled beef.

HORSERADISH SAUCE WITH CURRANTS (Russian)

Wash and scald a quarter of a pound of currants, then add them to a pint of stock with three ounces of grated horseradish and a little salt. Simmer gently for a quarter of an hour.

Use with boiled fresh beef.

HORSERADISH HOLLANDAISE SAUCE

To half a pint of Hollandaise Sauce (p. 27) add three level table-spoonfuls of grated horseradish and two tablespoonfuls of stiffly whisked double cream.

Use with boiled beef and poached or grilled fish.

HORSERADISH AND MUSTARD SAUCE (American)

3 tbs. butter; 2 tbs. flour; ½ pint white stock (p. 33); 1 tsp. chopped onion; 1 tsp. mixed English and French mustard; 1 tsp. horseradish; lemon juice; 2 tbs. double cream.

Melt the butter, stir in the flour, and make a sauce with the stock. When the sauce is smooth add salt and pepper, the chopped onion, mixed mustard and grated horseradish. Cook for twenty minutes, then strain and finish gradually with a little lemon juice and the thick cream.

Use with hamburgers.

HUNGARIAN SAUCE

½ lb. onions; 2 oz. lard; paprika pepper; 3 fl. oz. white wine; ½ pint thickened stock or Espagnole Sauce (p. 26); ½ pint sour cream.

Fry the chopped onions in the lard until they are browned, then add a large pinch of paprika pepper, the white wine, the thickened stock or

Espagnole Sauce, and the sour cream. Bring to the boil and keep warm until wanted.

See also Sauce Hongroise (p. 134).

Use with fish or veal.

INDIAN SAUCE 1

1 onion; 1 oz. butter; 1 tbs. curry powder; 2 tsp. flour; ¾ pint stock; 1 tsp. chutney; 1 cooking apple; salt; 1 tsp. lemon juice.

Fry the sliced onion brown in the butter, then add the curry powder and flour and cook gently for a quarter of an hour. Moisten now with the stock, bring to the boil, and add the chutney, the sliced cooking apple and a good pinch of salt, and simmer on for another twenty minutes. Then strain, reheat and finish with the lemon juice.

Use with curries.

INDIAN SAUCE 2

½ pint Espagnole Sauce (p. 26); 1 tsp. chopped Indian pickles; Worcestershire sauce; Harvey's sauce; glaze.

Heat the Espagnole Sauce, and add the chopped Indian pickles, ten drops of Worcestershire sauce, fifteen drops of Harvey's sauce and a good piece of glaze. Boil for ten minutes.

Use with salmon.

IRISH SAUCE

4 tbs. strong gravy; 4 chopped anchovies; 1 small piece horseradish; marjoram; parsley; mace; 1 clove; 6 peppercorns; nutmeg; 1 slice onion; 1 pint White Sauce (p. 24).

Put into a saucepan the gravy, anchovies, a small piece of horseradish, a smaller piece each of marjoram, parsley and mace, the clove, peppercorns, a tiny bit of nutmeg and the slice of onion. Simmer all these together for about quarter of an hour, when the liquid will be reduced by about half, then strain it into the White Sauce, mix and heat up, and serve.

Use with fish.

JELLIED MAYONNAISE SAUCE

To three quarters of a pint of Mayonnaise Sauce (p. 28), add, little by little, eight tablespoonfuls of cold melted thick jelly, meat or fish, according to the purpose for which the Mayonnaise is to be used.

Use for masking dishes.

JELLY WINE SAUCE

3 level dessertsp. melted butter; 3 level dessertsp. flour; salt; 2 tbs. red-currant jelly; 4 tbs. port wine; 2 tsp. lemon juice; 4 chopped maraschino cherries.

Mix the melted butter with the flour, moisten with a breakfastcupful of water, and cook, stirring, until thickened and the flour is cooked. Then add half a teaspoonful of salt, the red-currant jelly, port, lemon juice and maraschino cherries. Cook all together for a minute, stirring all the time, and serve hot.

Use with game and venison.

KIDNEY SAUCE

2 oz. ox kidney; ½ oz. butter; 1 dessertsp. flour; ½ pint stock or water.

Cut the ox kidney into small pieces and fry them for a few minutes in the butter. Sprinkle with the flour and brown slightly. Add the stock or water, season to taste, simmer gently for twenty minutes or so, then strain.

Use with grilled steak or kidney.

KING OF OUDE'S SAUCE

½ pint melted red-currant jelly; ¼ pint white vinegar; 2 tbs. port wine; 2 tbs. Harvey's sauce.

Shake the red-currant jelly in a bottle together with the white vinegar, port wine and Harvey's sauce. Serve cold.

Use with cold meat.

LEGHORN SAUCE (Sauce Livornaise)

3 hard-boiled egg yolks; ½ pint olive oil; nutmeg; pepper; 2 sieved and pounded anchovies (or anchovy essence or paste); ½ tsp. minced parsley; vinegar; tarragon vinegar.

Make a thick cream by crushing the hard-boiled egg yolks and diluting them with olive oil drop by drop, as for a Mayonnaise. Then stir in a pinch of grated nutmeg, a little pepper, the anchovies, minced parsley and vinegar and tarragon vinegar to taste.

Use with cold meat or chicken.

LEMON SAUCE I (Swedish)

1¾ oz. butter; 3 egg yolks; 8 tbs. cream; salt; sugar; grated peel and juice of ½ small lemon; 2 tbs. finely chopped parsley.

Heat the butter and add the egg yolks beaten in the cream, with a seasoning of salt and sugar to taste. Let this sauce thicken over a very low heat without boiling, then add the grated lemon peel and juice. Lastly add the finely chopped parsley, which has first been blanched for a few minutes in slightly salted boiling water, then dried.

Use with fish.

LEMON SAUCE 2

1 lemon; 1 liver of fowl or rabbit; ½ pint Béchamel Sauce (p. 24) or Melted-Butter Sauce (p. 96); salt; a little minced parsley or tarragon.

Peel the lemon, remove the pips and cut the flesh into dice. The lemon, the minced liver and Béchamel or Melted-Butter Sauce are then all cooked slowly together. Season with salt, and finish with a little minced parsley or tarragon.

Use with boiled fowl or rabbit.

LITTLETON SAUCE (American)

1 level tsp. flour; 1 level tsp. mustard; 3 tsp. melted butter; 3 tsp. vinegar; 3 egg yolks; salt and pepper; cayenne; 3 level tsp. red-currant jelly.

Mix together the flour and mustard and then add the melted butter, the vinegar, four fl. ounces of boiling water and three well-beaten egg yolks. Stir continuously in a double saucepan until the sauce thickens, then add salt, pepper and cayenne, and at the last the red-currant jelly divided into small bits. The sauce should not wait after the jelly and seasonings have been added.

Use with roast chicken or lamb.

LIVER SAUCE 1

1 anchovy; 1 chicken liver; parsley; lemon; butter; flour; cream.

Boil the anchovy and the chicken liver with a little parsley and a small piece of lemon in a little water until the anchovy is dissolved. Then remove the liver and mash it up finely; strain the liquid and add to this a little butter kneaded with flour, the liver, a very little lemon juice and a little cream. Bring to the boil and cook for a few minutes.

Use with boiled chicken.

LIVER SAUCE 2 (Czechoslovakian)

½ lb. liver; 1 onion; 1½ oz. butter; 3 tbs. flour; pepper; salt.

Cut the liver into small pieces. Fry the onion, finely sliced, until golden-brown in the butter, add the liver and cook for five minutes, stirring the while. Now add the flour, cook on for a minute or two, take the pan from the heat and add a teacupful of cold water. Mash and beat until the contents of the pan are smooth, then add a pint of hot water, with a seasoning of pepper, but no salt, and cook for five minutes longer. At the last season with salt; if the salt is added sooner the liver will harden.

Use with boiled chicken or rabbit.

LIVER AND PARSLEY SAUCE

Add to half a pint of Melted-Butter Sauce (p. 96), a cooked and finely chopped chicken or rabbit liver, and a tablespoonful of finely chopped parsley, with salt and pepper to taste.

Use as above.

Savoury Sauces

LOBSTER SAUCE I (Sauce Homard)

Add two ounces of Lobster Butter (p. 184) to three quarters of a pint of Cream Sauce (p. 62), season with a few drops of anchovy essence and garnish with little dice of lobster flesh.

Use with boiled turbot or similar prime fish.

LOBSTER SAUCE 2

1 hen lobster; butter; ½ pint fresh cream.

Take out the meat from a freshly boiled hen lobster, and cut it up into small dice. Mix the coral (the roe of the lobster) with them and put them into a saucepan with a piece of fresh butter and the fresh cream. Stir over the fire until the sauce is hot, and serve.

Use as above.

LOBSTER HOLLANDAISE SAUCE

To half a pint of Hollandaise Sauce (p. 27) add two tablespoonfuls of diced cooked lobster.

Use as above.

MAÎTRE D'HÔTEL SAUCE I

Add, at the last minute, to half a pint of Béchamel Sauce (p. 24), a teaspoonful of minced parsley, a squeeze of lemon and a little more salt and white pepper.

Use with poached fish.

MAÎTRE D'HÔTEL SAUCE 2

To half a pint of hot Hollandaise Sauce (p. 27) add a teaspoonful of chopped parsley, half an ounce of butter in small pieces, a little white pepper and some grated nutmeg.

Use as above.

MARTIN SAUCE

Make a Normandy Sauce (p. 102), omitting the lemon juice, and flavouring to taste with grated cheese.

Use with fish.

MAYONNAISE SAUCE

Basic sauce (see p. 28).

Mayonnaise Sauce Variations

Hors d'Œuvres. Various differently flavoured Mayonnaises can be made especially for garnishing hors d'œuvres. The purées used for this purpose are first pounded and mixed with a little Mayonnaise to assist even mixing, and an equal part or two thirds of the Mayonnaise is then added to them. Subjects for addition are the creamy parts of lobster or crab, shrimps or prawns, anchovies etc. as well as simple additions for flavouring only, such as anchovy essence, paprika pepper, tomato paste, hard-boiled egg yolks and curry powder.

Salads. The American kitchen is especially good at preparing salads and has created a large number of variations of sauces, both Mayonnaises and Vinaigrettes, with which to dress them. Those of Mayonnaise follow; the various Vinaigrettes will be found on pp. 174–177.

The quantities of the ingredients apply to eight tablespoons of the sauce. Spoonfuls are level.

Cheese Mayonnaise. Mix three teaspoonfuls of single cream with the Mayonnaise and fold in two tablespoonfuls of grated white cheese, seasoning with salt and paprika pepper.

Chutney Mayonnaise. Add three teaspoonfuls of chopped drained chutney.

Chilli Mayonnaise. Add four tablespoonfuls of mild chilli sauce, three dessertspoonfuls of vinegar, three teaspoonfuls of Worcestershire sauce and a teaspoonful and a half of chopped chives. (Pains should be taken to use the specially mild chilli sauce which can be obtained at good stores, otherwise the Mayonnaise will be disastrously inedible.)

Connelly Mayonnaise Sauce. Add a good tablespoonful of well drained and dried cold boiled rice.

Cream Mayonnaise Sauce. Fold in three tablespoonfuls of double cream, well whipped.
See also Mayonnaise Chantilly (p. 96).

Cream Cheese Mayonnaise Sauce. Cream three ounces of cream cheese with three dessertspoonfuls of Camembert or Roquefort cheese, and mix gradually with the Mayonnaise, thinning down with cream as desired.

Crisp Mayonnaise Sauce. Add two tablespoonfuls of crisp chopped raw celery and cucumber mixed together and two or three teaspoonfuls of double fresh or sour cream.

Green Mayonnaise Sauce. Pound four tablespoonfuls of watercress and two tablespoonfuls of parsley in a mortar, squeeze through a cloth and use the liquid to colour the Mayonnaise. Spinach may be added to the ingredients when pounding.

Ham Mayonnaise Sauce. Add four tablespoonfuls of tomato juice and three dessertspoonfuls of finely chopped cooked ham.

Honey Cream Mayonnaise Sauce. Add a quarter of a teaspoonful of dry mustard mixed with three teaspoonfuls of honey and half a teaspoon of lemon juice, and fold in quarter of a pint of whipped cream.

Mustard Cream Mayonnaise Sauce. Add four tablespoonfuls of made mustard (preferably French) and then fold in quarter of a pint of whipped double cream.

Pickle Mayonnaise Sauce. Add a teaspoonful and a half each of tomato ketchup and minced parsley and three teaspoonfuls each of minced sweet pickle, pickled cucumber and pickled beetroot.

Pimento Cheese Mayonnaise Sauce. Add two tablespoonfuls of pimento cheese (a spread which may be purchased commercially) or cream cheese mashed with finely minced red sweet peppers, an extra touch of salt and a finely chopped hard-boiled egg.

Pimento Mustard Mayonnaise Sauce. Add three dessertspoonfuls of minced red sweet peppers, a quarter of a teaspoonful of dry mustard and a little paprika pepper. Thin with a teaspoonful of vinegar and a little cream.

Piquant Mayonnaise Sauce. 1. Add three teaspoonfuls each of finely chopped green olives and drained pickles.
    2. First rub the mixing bowl with a cut clove of garlic, then to the Mayonnaise base add three dessertspoonfuls each of minced red and green sweet peppers and two tablespoonfuls each of minced celery, pickled cucumber, mild chilli sauce and tomato ketchup.

Red Mayonnaise Sauce. Colour the Mayonnaise to taste with very red tomato purée or paste. If for fish, use finely sieved or pounded lobster coral.

Russian Mayonnaise Sauce. Add two teaspoonfuls each of chopped red and green sweet peppers and chives, half a teaspoonful of paprika pepper, two tablespoonfuls of mild chilli sauce and a sieved hard-boiled egg yolk.

Savoury Mayonnaise Sauce. Add a good pinch each of dry mustard, paprika pepper and Worcestershire sauce.

Further Mayonnaise Sauce Variations

Aïoli	Casanova Mayonnaise
Asparagus Mayonnaise	Chives Mayonnaise
Banana Nut Mayonnaise	Cucumber Mayonnaise
Béchamel Mayonnaise	Epicurean Sauce
Cambridge Sauce	Gloucester Sauce

Green Pea Mayonnaise
Guaymas Sauce
Jellied Mayonnaise
Marmalade Mayonnaise
Mayonnaise, cleared
Mayonnaise, hot
Mayonnaise, whisked
Mayonnaise Chantilly
Mousseline Sauce 2
Paolo Mayonnaise
Ravigote Mayonnaise
Sauce Bohémienne
Sauce Gribiche

Sauce Italienne
Sauce Mayonnaise Escoffier
Sauce Mousquetaire
Sauce Niçoise
Sauce Provençale, froide
Sauce Rémoulade
Sauce Russe
Sauce Suédoise
Sauce Tartare
Sauce Tyrolienne 3
Sauce Vincent
Thousand Island Dressing

MAYONNAISE SAUCE (Cleared)

Add gradually to a pint and a half of Mayonnaise Sauce (p. 28) half a
pint of cold and rather firm melting aspic jelly.

Use for coating cold entrées of fish.

MAYONNAISE SAUCE (Whisked)

*¾ pint melted aspic jelly; ⅔ pint Mayonnaise (p. 28); 1 tbs. tarragon
vinegar; 1 tbs. grated horseradish.*

Put into a bowl the melted aspic jelly, Mayonnaise Sauce, tarragon
vinegar and grated horseradish. Mix up the whole, put the basin on
ice, and whisk gently until the contents get very frothy. Stop whisking as soon as the sauce begins to solidify.

Use principally for vegetable salads.

MAYONNAISE SAUCE (Hot) (American)

*2 egg yolks; 3 dessertsp. olive oil; 3 tsp. vinegar; salt; cayenne; 1 level tsp.
finely chopped parsley.*

Put the egg yolks into a basin, and add to them very slowly the olive
oil. Pour on gradually the vinegar and four tablespoonfuls of hot
water, and cook in a double saucepan, stirring all the time, until it

thickens. Then season with salt and a little cayenne, and add at the last the finely chopped parsley.

Use with fish.

MAYONNAISE CHANTILLY SAUCE

This is Mayonnaise Sauce (p. 28) mixed with a little lightly whipped cream.

Use as for Mayonnaise.

MELTED BUTTER (Beurre Fondu)

This preparation should consist of butter, only just melted and combined with a little table salt and a few drops of lemon juice. It should therefore be prepared only at the last minute; for, should it wait and be allowed to clarify, besides losing its flavour it will be found to disagree with certain people.

Use principally as a fish sauce.

MELTED-BUTTER SAUCE

1 oz. butter; ¾ oz. flour; salt and pepper.

This is the traditional English sauce, a White Sauce made with water instead of milk. Melt the butter and stir in the flour. Cook for three or four minutes, and then dilute with half a pint of hot but not boiling water, bringing to the boil to thicken, and seasoning with salt and pepper.

Use for any purpose for which white sauce is used.

MEXICAN SAUCE

1 onion; butter; 1 red sweet pepper; 1 green sweet pepper; 2 tomatoes; 1 clove garlic; 1 tsp. Worcestershire sauce; ¼ tsp. celery salt.

Chop up the onion finely and stew it in a little butter for five minutes. Then add the red and green sweet peppers, both chopped and seeds removed, the peeled tomatoes cut in slices, the garlic, Worcestershire sauce and celery salt. Simmer for a quarter of an hour, take out the clove of garlic, correct the seasoning and serve.

Excellent sauce in which to warm up cold meat.

MICHAEL KELLY'S SAUCE

1 tsp. mustard; 1 tsp. brown sugar; 1 tsp. black pepper; 1 tbs. garlic vinegar; ½ pint melted butter.

Mix together the mustard, brown sugar and black pepper with the garlic vinegar. Have ready the melted butter, and while it is hot, stir the vinegar mixture into it.

Use with boiled calf's head, cow-heel or tripe.

MICHAEL KELLY'S SHARP SAUCE

1 tsp. capers; 1 tbs. parsley; 3 hard-boiled egg yolks; 1 tbs. made mustard; 6 anchovies; 1 shallot; 1 tbs. vinegar; 2 tbs. salad oil; cayenne; ½ pint good gravy.

Pound the capers; mince the parsley; mix the yolks with the mustard; bone and pound up the anchovies. Mix these ingredients all together and pound them in a mortar with the minced shallot and vinegar and salad oil. Season with a little cayenne pepper, and mix well with the gravy. Pass the whole through a sieve and make hot before sending to table.

Use as above.

MILANAISE SAUCE

4 oz. onions; 1 oz. butter; salt; 1 tbs. boiled rice or pearl barley; ½ pint broth; 1 tbs. finely grated cheese (Parmesan if possible); ½ pint white sauce (p. 24).

Put the onions, blanched and cut up, into a saucepan with the butter, a saltspoonful of salt and a drop of water. Add the boiled rice or pearl barley, and moisten with the broth. Let all cook slowly and, when the onions are done, add the grated cheese. Stir until the cheese melts, pass through a sieve, and add it to the White Sauce.

Use with anything that cheese or onion goes with.

MILK GRAVY (American)

4 thin rashers bacon; flour; cream; salt and pepper; chopped parsley.

Put the bacon into a pan and bake in the oven until the rashers are crisp. Then take them out. Pour away all but two and a half tablespoonfuls of the fat in the pan, then put the pan on the heat and dredge in enough flour to make your sauce. Mix well, stirring all the time, and before the flour begins to brown, pour in some cream off the top of the milk. Let this boil up several times, and add salt if necessary, pepper and chopped parsley.

Use with roast chicken.

MINT SAUCE I

2 tbs. chopped mint; 3–4 tsp. sugar; ¼ pint vinegar.

Wash and dry the fresh mint thoroughly, chop it up very finely, add the sugar and pour over it an eighth of a pint of boiling water, which will keep the mint a good green. Then add the vinegar and serve cold.

Use with roast lamb.

MINT SAUCE 2 (Créole)

1 handful mint; 1 tsp. tarragon vinegar; 1 tsp. sugar; 1 pint beef stock.

Put a good handful of freshly chopped mint into a basin and add the tarragon vinegar and the sugar. Then add a pint of good beef stock and let the sauce warm through in a bain-marie without boiling, for if it boils the mint will be bitter. Serve hot.

Use as above.

MOCK HOLLANDAISE SAUCE

Just before serving, stir into half a pint of White Sauce (p. 24) two egg yolks, four level tablespoonfuls of butter, a tablespoonful at a time, and lastly three teaspoonfuls of lemon juice.

Use as for Hollandaise Sauce.

MONTEBELLO SAUCE

Heat together very carefully, without boiling, equal parts of Tomato

Sauce (p. 170), and Béarnaise Sauce (p. 121), adding two or three sliced truffles at the last.

Use with roast chicken.

MOUSSELINE SAUCE 1 (Hot)

1 good handful spinach or watercress; 1 tbs. cream; 1 dessertsp. tarragon vinegar; salt and pepper; 2 egg yolks.

Pound the spinach or watercress in a mortar and rub it through a fine sieve. Put this purée into a saucepan with the cream, tarragon vinegar, salt, pepper and egg yolks, and whisk over the heat until it is light and frothy.

Use with fish or roast chicken.

MOUSSELINE SAUCE 2 (Cold)

Prepare the spinach or watercress as above, and mix it with a quarter of a pint of Mayonnaise Sauce (p. 28). Whip an eighth of a pint of cream stiffly, and add the flavoured Mayonnaise to it very lightly.

Use with salmon and other fish.

MUSHROOM SAUCE 1 (White)

Béchamel Sauce (p. 24); white stock (p. 33); mushroom trimmings; 4 oz. bottled champignons; 2–3 tbs. white wine.

Boil together equal parts of Béchamel Sauce and white stock with a handful of mushroom trimmings. When reduced by a third, sieve the sauce, and for each half pint of this sauce add four ounces of sliced bottled champignons, and two or three tablespoonfuls of white wine. Just bring to the boil, and serve.

Use with fish, eggs, poultry, vegetables.

MUSHROOM SAUCE 2 (Swedish)

¼ lb. fresh mushrooms; 1½ tbs. butter; 2 tbs. flour; 1 scant pint gravy or fish stock (p. 34); 2 tbs. mushroom cooking liquor (p. 37); Madeira.

Peel and cut the mushrooms into slices, and brown them in the butter. Press the mushrooms against the side of the pan and take them out; add the flour to the butter and stir and cook for two minutes. Then add the gravy and mushroom cooking liquor, and cook on for another ten minutes. Then add the mushroom slices and seasoning to taste, and heat through again. A touch of Madeira may be added if liked.

If the sauce is for fish, fish stock should be used instead of gravy.

Use with roast chicken or fish.

MUSSEL SAUCE

A quarter of a pint of chopped shelled cooked mussels are added to a pint of Melted-Butter Sauce, with a teaspoonful of lemon juice and salt and pepper to taste.

Use with boiled fish.

MUSTARD SAUCE I

1 oz. dripping; ½ oz. flour; ¼ pint fish stock (p. 34); 1 tsp. dry mustard; 1–2 tbs. vinegar; salt and pepper; cayenne; cream.

Melt the dripping and mix in the flour; add the fish stock and stir until the sauce thickens. Mix the dry mustard with the vinegar, add the sauce to this and bring it to the boil again. Season with salt, pepper, and perhaps a touch of cayenne and finish with a little cream.

Use with herrings and other fish.

MUSTARD SAUCE 2

Melted-Butter Sauce (p. 96); 1 tsp. French or English mustard; 1 dessertsp. chilli vinegar; anchovy essence; soft herring roes.

Add to some Melted-Butter Sauce the mustard, the chilli vinegar and a little anchovy essence, and make hot. The soft roes may be mashed and sieved (after being cooked) and amalgamated with the sauce.

Use with broiled or fried herrings.

MUSTARD SAUCE 3 (American)

3 level tsp. cornflour; ¾ pint cream; 4 tbs. sugar; 1 tsp. salt; 2 egg yolks; 2 level dessertsp. dry mustard; 8 fl. oz. vinegar.

Mix the cornflour in a little of the cream, bring the rest to the boil in a double saucepan, add the cornflour to this, and cook until thick. Now add the sugar and salt. Beat up the egg yolks with the dry mustard, add this to the cream, and let the sauce thicken. Lastly add the vinegar and cook for a minute longer, stirring all the time. Serve hot or cold.

Use with herrings and other fish.

MUSTARD SAUCE WITH CREAM

Put three tablespoonfuls of dry mustard into a basin with a little salt, pepper and a few drops of lemon juice. Mix well together and add, little by little, the necessary amount of very fresh cream: less if you want a strong mustard flavour, more if you wish the sauce to be mild.

Use with salads.

NEAPOLITAN SAUCE

3 shallots; juice of 1 lemon; ½ pint fish stock (p. 34); ground mace; cayenne; 1 clove; ½ bayleaf; 1 oz. butter; 1 tbs. flour; ¼ tsp. anchovy essence; 1 dessertsp. capers.

Chop up the shallots finely and put them into a saucepan with the lemon juice. Stir over a low heat for a few minutes, then add the fish stock, a pinch each of ground mace and cayenne pepper, one clove and half a bayleaf. Bring to the boil, simmer for twenty minutes and then strain. In another saucepan make a white roux (p. 23) with the butter and flour, add the sauce gradually and bring to the boil, simmering for a few minutes. At the last add the anchovy essence and capers.

Use with boiled fish.

NEWCASTLE FISH SAUCE

3 tbs. vinegar; 3 tbs. strong gravy; 3–4 anchovies; ½ lb. creamed butter; ketchup.

Boil together the vinegar, gravy and anchovies cut in pieces, until the liquid is reduced to one tablespoonful; then strain it off and add the creamed butter and a spoonful of ketchup to taste. Boil all together just before you serve it.

NORMANDY SAUCE (American)

3 level dessertsp. butter; 2 level tbs. flour; 8 fl. oz. fish stock (p. 34); 3 tbs. double cream; 3 egg yolks; salt and pepper; cayenne; 3 tsp. lemon juice.

Make a white roux (p. 23) with the butter and flour, and moisten with the fish stock and double cream. Bring to the boil, and just before serving, add the slightly beaten egg yolks and a seasoning of salt, pepper, cayenne and lemon juice.

See also Sauce Normande (p. 143).

Use with fish, eggs and vegetables.

OLIVE SAUCE 1

Bind three quarters of a pint of White Sauce (p. 24) with a slightly beaten egg and an eighth of a pint of single cream, then add four tablespoonfuls of chopped black olives.

Use with sweetbreads, tongue or boiled beef.

OLIVE SAUCE 2

1 tbs. chopped carrot; 1 tbs. chopped onion; 1 tbs. butter; 1 tbs. flour; ½ pint well-flavoured brown stock (p. 32); salt and pepper; 1 clove; 20 olives.

Brown the chopped carrot and onion in the butter, add the flour and let that brown too. Moisten with the stock, season with salt, pepper and one clove, simmer for twenty minutes, and then strain. Stone the olives, leaving the flesh in one piece, and boil them in a little water for half an hour. Then add them to the sauce and cook together for five minutes.

Use with duck.

OLIVE-ALMOND SAUCE (American)

To half a pint of Béchamel Sauce (p. 24) add five tablespoonfuls of blanched and shredded almonds, eight stoned and quartered olives, a teaspoonful and a half of lemon juice and a dash of cayenne pepper.

Use with boiled or baked fish or chicken entrées.

OLIVERA SAUCE (American)

12 sliced mushrooms; 2 tbs. butter; 3 level dessertsp. flour; ¾ pint stock; 4 tbs. picked shrimps; ¼ tsp. Worcestershire sauce; salt and pepper; sherry.

Toss the mushrooms into the butter, take them out when browned and stir the flour into the butter. Then add the stock, and cook until smooth and thick. Put back the mushrooms, and add the shrimps, Worcestershire sauce and salt and pepper to taste. A little sherry may be added, if desired.

Use with fish.

ONION SAUCE I

½ lb. onions; 1 pint White Sauce (p. 24); nutmeg.

Blanch the onions, then put them into cold water with a little salt and cook them for about an hour or until they are quite tender. Then drain and chop them finely, and add them to the White Sauce. Add a little nutmeg to the seasoning.

Use with roast lamb.

ONION SAUCE 2 (Russian)

3–4 large onions; fat; 1 tbs. flour; salt and pepper; 1 dessertsp. vinegar.

Brown the chopped onions in a little fat, thicken with the flour and moisten with four fl. ounces of water. Cook until the sauce is thick and creamy, then add salt and pepper to taste and the vinegar.

Use with boiled fish.

ORANGE SAUCE I

2 oranges; 1 lemon; ½ pint rich brown gravy; salt and pepper.

Cut the red part of the rind of an orange into thin match-like strips and pour boiling water on them. Boil them for five minutes and then drain them. Now add to this peel the juice of two oranges and of one lemon, and the rich brown gravy. Season with salt and pepper to taste, heat through and serve.

Use with wild duck or game.

ORANGE SAUCE 2 (American)

1 tbs. butter; 1 tbs. flour; 2 tbs. sugar; 2 tbs. sultanas; 1 orange.

Melt the butter, stir in the flour, moisten with a scant half pint of water and add the sugar and sultanas. Cook until clear, then add the grated rind and strained juice of an orange. Serve hot.

Use with fish or meat.

ORANGE SAUCE 3

2 oranges; 1 oz. butter; 1 oz. flour; ½ pint stock or gravy; salt and pepper.

Make an infusion (see p. 37) from the thinly peeled rind of two oranges and let it soak for ten minutes. Now make a sauce with the butter, flour, and stock or gravy, and cook for a quarter of an hour or so, letting it reduce a little. Add a tablespoonful of the infusion from the orange rinds and the juice of the two oranges, season with salt and pepper, and heat through to serve.

Use with wild duck or game.

ORANGE SAUCE 4

2 onions; ham; 1 orange; cayenne; gravy; 2 tbs. port wine; 1 lemon.

Chop up the onions and a little bit of raw ham or gammon, and mix them with the finely grated rind of the orange and a little cayenne pepper. Just cover these with good gravy (the gravy from the bird is best), add the port wine and simmer for five minutes. Then add the juice of the orange and the lemon, sieve very finely and serve.

Use with duck and game.

ORANGE SAUCE 5 (Cold) (American)

4 level tbs. red-currant jelly; 2 level tbs. sugar; 2 oranges; lemon juice; salt; cayenne.

Put the red-currant jelly into a bowl with the sugar and the grated rind of two oranges, and beat them for five minutes. Then add three dessertspoonfuls each of orange and lemon juice, a quarter of a level teaspoonful of salt and half as much cayenne pepper. Stir until all is well blended.

Use with duck, pork, game.

ORANGE MINT SAUCE

4 fl. oz. orange juice; 4 fl. oz. lemon juice; mint; pineapple; 1 tbs. castor sugar.

Mix together the orange juice, lemon juice, some finely chopped mint, two tablespoonfuls of well-drained shredded pineapple and the castor sugar. Leave in a warm place for about an hour and stir well.

Use with lamb.

OXFORD SAUCE

See Cumberland Sauce (p. 65), the only difference being that the orange and lemon rinds are finely chopped or grated and that they are slightly less in quantity.

Use with game (e.g. venison), cold pork, ham.

OYSTER SAUCE 1 (Sauce aux Huîtres)

To three quarters of a pint of White Wine Sauce (p. 179) add a dozen poached and bearded oysters, as well as their cooking liquor reduced and passed through a fine cloth.

Use with turbot or other prime white fish, or boiled chicken.

OYSTER SAUCE 2 (Sauce aux Huîtres)

This is a Sauce Normande (p. 143) flavoured with oyster liquor, and garnished with lightly-poached bearded oysters.

Use as above.

OYSTER SAUCE 3

1 pint oysters; 2 oz. butter; 2 oz. flour; ½ pint milk; salt and pepper; lemon juice.

Open a pint of oysters, drain their liquor into a saucepan, remove their beards, and heat them gently through in the liquor. Have ready a thick White Sauce (p. 24) made with the butter, flour and milk. Strain and mix the oyster liquor with this, and then add the oysters themselves, whole or cut in pieces, and reheat the sauce without letting it boil. Finish with salt and pepper and a dash of lemon.

Use with boiled fowl or turkey.

PAOLO MAYONNAISE SAUCE (American)

This is a Mayonnaise Sauce (p. 28) to which have been added a table-spoonful of capers, the same of chopped sweet pickle, a chopped hard-boiled egg and a teaspoonful each of lime juice and chopped parsley.

Use as for Mayonnaise.

PAPRIKA SAUCE 1

2 rashers bacon; 1 onion; butter or lard; paprika pepper; 1 pint sour milk; flour; salt and pepper.

Chop up the bacon with the onion and fry them in butter or lard until browned. Season with paprika pepper to taste. Boil the sour milk until it thickens, then thicken it further with a little flour and season it with salt and pepper. Add the onion and bacon mixture, cook a little together, strain and serve.

Use with fish or meat.

PAPRIKA SAUCE 2

1 large onion; butter; paprika pepper; flour; 1 ripe red tomato; salt and pepper; ½ pint sour cream.

Chop up the onion and stew it in a little butter until soft. Add as much paprika pepper as your taste dictates and enough flour to make the sauce the right consistency. Add the finely chopped tomato. Cook a little with the lid on, and season with salt and pepper. Then add the sour cream, and cook on until the sauce thickens as you would wish. Strain if you like.

Use as above.

PAPRIKA SAUCE 3 (Hungarian)

4 oz. chopped onion; 2 oz. lard; 2 oz. flour; ½ tsp. paprika pepper; salt; ½ pint stock; 1 dessertsp. vinegar; tomato purée or cream.

Fry the chopped onion lightly in the lard, stir in the flour and paprika pepper, season with salt and moisten with the warm stock and vinegar. Cook for twenty minutes, then thicken with either a few spoonfuls of tomato purée or a small cupful of double cream.

Use as above.

PAPRIKA SAUCE 4 (Rose)

See Sauce Curry à la Crème (p. 129) and make in the same way, substituting Hungarian paprika pepper for the curry powder.

Use as above.

PARSLEY SAUCE

1 oz. butter; 1 oz. flour; ¼ pint cream; 1 pint veal stock (p. 32); 2 tbs. chopped parsley.

Make a white roux (p. 23) with the butter and flour, and moisten smoothly with the cream. Bring the veal stock to the boil and add this gradually to the thickened cream, with the chopped parsley. Heat up in a double saucepan for a quarter of an hour, but do not allow the sauce to boil.

Use with fish, white meat, poultry, eggs or vegetables.

PEANUT BUTTER SAUCE

3 dessertsp. butter; 3 dessertsp. peanut butter; 3 tbs. flour; ¾ pint chicken stock (p. 33); salt and pepper.

Lightly brown the butter, add the peanut butter and when well mixed, stir in the flour. Let this brown and then gradually add the chicken stock. Stir while it thickens, then season with salt and pepper, and serve.

Use with roast chicken.

PEG WOFFINGTON SAUCE

½ pint cooking liquor from white fish poached with white wine; ¼ pint cream; 1 tbs. walnut ketchup; ½ tbs. anchovy essence; butter; flour; red pepper.

Take the cooking liquor of the white fish and strain; then add to it the cream, walnut ketchup and anchovy essence. Boil all together, and finish with a piece of butter the size of a walnut rolled in flour with a suspicion of red pepper.

Use with poached fish.

PICKLE SAUCE (Créole)

To an ordinary White Sauce (p. 24), add, just before serving, some chopped pickled gherkins or any other vinegar pickle you like, in proportion according to your taste. Do not, however, add any of the pickle liquid.

Use with meat.

PICKLED WALNUT SAUCE

2 oz. butter; 2 tbs. pickled-walnut liquor; 3–4 pickled walnuts; salt and pepper.

Melt butter in a small saucepan, and add to it the pickled-walnut liquor and the roughly chopped pickled walnuts. Season with salt and pepper to taste and serve very hot.

Use with roast lamb or venison.

PIMENTO SAUCE

2 tbs. butter; 2 tbs. flour; ½ pint milk; salt and pepper; ¼ pint cream; ¼ pint pimento purée.

Make a White Sauce (p. 24) with the butter, flour and milk, seasoning it with salt and pepper. Add to this the cream and the pimento purée, which is made by rubbing tinned sweet red peppers through a fine sieve. Heat through and serve.

Use with fish or veal.

PIMENTO AND GREEN PEPPER SAUCE

Fry two chopped green peppers slightly in butter before adding flour and making a sauce with milk. Then add an equal amount of chopped red sweet peppers and season rather highly.

Use with fish or veal.

PIMENTO-PARSLEY SAUCE (American)

To half a pint of White Sauce (p. 24) add three to four tablespoonfuls of diced sweet red pepper and three to four dessertspoonfuls of chopped parsley.

Use with boiled fish or egg dishes.

PINEAPPLE CREAM SAUCE (American)

To half a pint of Cream Sauce (p. 62) add four tablespoonfuls of cream and three tablespoonfuls of drained crushed pineapple.

Use with fish.

PIQUANT SAUCE

2 hard-boiled egg yolks; 1 oz. grated horseradish; ½ oz. salt; 1 tbs. made mustard; 1 shallot; 1 tsp. celery seed; cayenne; 1 wineglass oil; 2 wineglasses tarragon or horseradish vinegar.

Pound together the egg yolks, grated horseradish, salt, made mustard, minced shallot, celery seed and a small quantity of cayenne pepper. Add the oil gradually with the tarragon or horseradish vinegar. Set it over a gentle heat and stir with a wooden spoon until it is like thick cream, then let it get cold.

Use as for Mayonnaise.

POIVRADE SAUCE

2 oz. butter; ½ lb. raw mirepoix (p. 36); ⅛ pint vinegar; ½ pint marinade (p. 35); ½ pint Espagnole Sauce (p. 26); peppercorns.

Heat an ounce of butter in a stewpan, and put in the raw mirepoix. Fry the vegetables until they are well-browned; moisten with the vinegar and half the marinade from the meat and reduce to two thirds. Add the Espagnole Sauce and cook for three quarters of an hour. Ten minutes before straining the sauce, put in a few crushed peppercorns. If the pepper is put in the sauce earlier, it may make it bitter. Now pass the sauce through a strainer, pressing the aromatics, add a further quarter of a pint of marinade. Return to the heat and simmer for fifteen minutes, skimming the top from time to time. Strain again through a fine sieve and finish the sauce, when ready for dishing, with an ounce of butter.

Serve with meat (particularly marinaded meat) or game.

PORTARLINGTON SAUCE

¼ pint good Brown Sauce (p. 26); 1 glass red wine; 1 tbs. red-currant jelly; glaze; cayenne; lemon juice.

Mix the Brown Sauce, red wine, red-currant jelly, a piece of glaze the size of a walnut, a grain of cayenne pepper and a squeeze of lemon. Heat through to serve.

Use with croquettes of hare or other game.

PORT WINE SAUCE

Put into a small saucepan and bring to the boil half a pint of gravy from the meat, a small glass of port wine, a teaspoonful of red-currant jelly and a few drops of lemon juice.

Use with venison, game or mutton.

PRUNE SAUCE I

1 lb. small prunes; 2 lemons; 4 blades mace; 2 doz. whole cloves; 1 tsp. whole allspice; 1 peppercorn; ½ lb. sugar; 8 tbs. cider vinegar.

Wash the prunes and put them in plenty of cold water with the juice of the lemons and their thin yellow peel, the mace, cloves and allspice, reinforced with a single peppercorn. Cook for two hours, simmering gently and filling up as the water wastes. Then put in the sugar and simmer another hour until the syrup is thick and rich. Then add the cider vinegar, let it boil for five minutes, and your sauce is done.

Use with sucking pig and roast pork.

PRUNE SAUCE 2

Boil a pound of prunes in half a pint of water until they are soft, then sweeten them with a tablespoonful of moist sugar, and flavour with a tablespoonful of brandy. Rub the sauce through a sieve, and serve.

Use with sucking pig, mutton or venison.

RAGÚ SAUCE ALLA BOLOGNESE (Italian)

10 oz. lean raw beef; 4 oz. streaky green bacon; 1 onion; 1 carrot; 1 stick celery; 2 oz. butter; salt and pepper; 1–2 cloves; about 1½ pints stock or water; 1 tbs. Tomato Sauce (p. 170); ¼ pint cream.

Put through the mincing-machine the beef, bacon, onion, carrot and celery, then brown them all in the butter, adding salt and pepper and the cloves. Moisten with half a pint of the stock or water, simmer for twenty minutes, and add another half-pint of the chosen liquid and the Tomato Sauce. Simmer until the liquid is reduced and then barely cover with more stock, bring to the boil and simmer on gently for a couple of hours. Stir in the cream just before serving.

Principally used for pastas such as tagliatelle, spaghetti and macaroni.

RAISIN SAUCE 1 (American)

¼ pint water in which ham or tongue has been boiled; 4 oz. brown sugar; 3 dessertsp. chopped raisins; ½ lemon; 1 tsp. butter.

Put into the saucepan the water, brown sugar, chopped raisins, the juice of half a lemon and the butter. Cook gently until the sauce thickens, then add the grated rind of the lemon-half, and the sauce is ready.

Use with ham or tongue.

RAISIN SAUCE 2 (American)

3 tbs. brown sugar; 1 tsp. dry mustard; 1 tbs. flour; 2 tbs. vinegar; lemon; 2 tbs. seedless raisins.

Mix together in a saucepan the brown sugar, dry mustard and flour. Blend in the vinegar gradually. Then add two tablespoonfuls of lemon juice and a quarter of a teaspoonful of finely grated lemon rind, and finally the seedless raisins and three quarters of a pint of water. Cook over a low heat until the sauce is thick and clear, stirring a good deal.

Use with ham or bacon.

RAISIN SAUCE 3

3 tbs. brown sugar; 1½ level tsp. each dry mustard and flour; 1 tbs. seeded or seedless raisins; 4 tbs. vinegar.

Mix together the brown sugar, dry mustard and flour, then add the raisins, vinegar and three quarters of a pint of water. Cook all together until you have a syrup of the right consistency.

Use with ham.

RAISIN SAUCE 4

6 oz. sugar; 6 tbs. raisins; 3 level dessertsp. butter; 2 tbs. vinegar; 1½ tsp. Worcestershire sauce; ½ level tsp. salt; ¼ level tsp. powdered cloves; ⅛ level tsp. pepper; 1 pinch mace; 2 tbs. red-currant jelly.

Cook the sugar in four fl. ounces water for five minutes, then add the raisins, seeded or cut in bits, the butter, vinegar, Worcestershire sauce, salt, powdered cloves, pepper, mace and red-currant or other suitable jelly. Cook until the jelly has dissolved, and the sauce is ready.

Use with ham.

RAVIGOTE MAYONNAISE SAUCE (American)

3 tsp. cooked spinach; 2 tsp. capers; ¼ small onion; 2 anchovy fillets; 3 dessertsp. each watercress and parsley; 6 tbs. Mayonnaise (p. 28).

Chop and mix together the spinach, capers, onion, anchovy fillets, watercress and parsley. Pound together and then rub through a fine sieve. Add to the Mayonnaise Sauce.

Use with fish and vegetable salads.

RED CHILLI SAUCE (American)

5 ripe tomatoes; 1 small onion; 2 red chilli peppers; 2 tbs. lard or bacon fat; 2 cloves garlic; salt and pepper; 1 sprig thyme; 1 leaf sage; 1 tbs. chopped parsley.

Peel the tomatoes and put them with the onion and chilli peppers through the mincing-machine. Heat the lard or bacon fat in a pan, add the tomato mixture and two mashed cloves of garlic, salt and pepper and the herbs, and cook slowly for fifteen minutes or longer, according to how thick you wish the sauce to be. Take out the thyme and the sage leaf before serving.

Use with barbecued poultry or meat.

RED-CURRANT MINT SAUCE

Separate a teacupful of red-currant jelly into small pieces. Add a tablespoonful of chopped fresh mint and just a little less of grated orange rind. Mix together but do not beat. Serve cold.

Use with roast lamb.

RÉMOULADE SAUCE I

See Sauce Rémoulade (p. 149).

Use as for Mayonnaise.

RÉMOULADE SAUCE 2

2 shallots; 1 small onion; chervil; parsley; salt and pepper; made mustard; oil; vinegar.

Put into a basin the shallots, onion, and some chervil and parsley, all finely chopped. Then add salt, pepper and made mustard to taste, and alternately stir in enough oil and vinegar (three parts oil to one of vinegar), to make your sauce.

Use as for Mayonnaise.

RICHELIEU SAUCE (Francatelli)

4 onions; a few roast game bones; 1 oz. flour; 1 glass sherry; ½ pint good stock; pepper and salt; glaze.

Peel, slice and fry the onions, add the roast game bones chopped fine, and the flour; mix well together, moisten with the sherry and stock, add a little pepper and salt, and a bit of glaze. Stir over the fire for a quarter of an hour, then rub through a hair-sieve, and keep hot in a small stewpan for use.

Use with roast game.

RIO GRANDE SAUCE (American)

1 onion; 2 tbs. butter; 1 red and 1 green sweet pepper; 2 tomatoes; 1 clove garlic; 1 tsp. Worcestershire sauce; 1 tsp. chilli powder; salt.

Mince the onion and stew it gently in the butter. Chop the peppers and add them with the peeled and chopped tomatoes to the onion. Simmer the whole for a quarter of an hour, then add the garlic, very finely chopped, the Worcestershire sauce and the chilli powder, with a seasoning of salt. Serve hot.

Use with boiled or grilled fish.

ROE SAUCE

½ lb. fresh cod's roe; 1 tsp. made mustard; 1 tsp. anchovy essence; 1 dessertsp. vinegar; ½ pint Melted-Butter Sauce (p. 96).

Cook the cod's roe in a little water, then skin it and crush it with the back of a wooden spoon, adding the mustard, anchovy essence and vinegar. Mix well and then stir the mixture into the Melted-Butter

Sauce, season to taste, simmer gently for a quarter of an hour, then strain and serve.

Use with boiled fish.

RUSSIAN SAUCE (American)

½ pint *Velouté Sauce* (p. 24); ½ level tsp. each *chopped chives and made mustard; 1 level tsp. grated horseradish; 4 tbs. cream; 1 tsp. lemon juice.*

Add to the Velouté Sauce the chives, mustard and grated horseradish. Cook together for two minutes, then add the cream and lemon juice. Heat up to serve, but without boiling.

Use with lobster, fish or roast chicken.

RUSSIAN OYSTER SAUCE (American)

12 oysters; a little chicken stock (p. 33); 2 level tbs. butter; flour; 1¼ pints cream; 2 egg yolks; 1½ tsp. vinegar; 2 tsp. lemon juice; 3 level dessertsp. capers; 3 level tsp. grated horseradish; salt and pepper.

Chop up the oysters, and poach them for five minutes in just enough water to cover. Strain off the liquid, and make this up to half a pint by adding chicken stock. Make a white roux (p. 23) with the butter and just over three level tablespoonfuls of flour, and moisten this with the oyster liquid, stock and cream. Bring to the boil, and add the chopped oysters, egg yolks, vinegar, lemon juice, capers, grated horseradish, and salt and pepper to taste.

Use with boiled turbot.

SAFFRON SAUCE (Sauce au Safran)

Make as a Béchamel Sauce (p. 24), adding when mixing a pinch of red saffron powder, or an infusion of saffron threads in water, the quantity according to your taste. Finish with a little butter.

Use as for Bread Sauce.

SAGE AND ONION SAUCE

2 tbs. butter; 2 minced onions; ½ pint brown stock (p. 32); 1 tsp. chopped sage; 2 tbs. breadcrumbs.

Melt the butter in a saucepan, and lightly brown the onions in it. Add the stock, bring to the boil, and then add the finely chopped sage leaves and breadcrumbs, and season to taste. Serve with roast pork, adding a tablespoonful or two of the gravy to the sauce at the last minute.

Use with duck or pork.

SALMIS SAUCE (English)

2 shallots; 1 tbs. oil; 1 bayleaf; 1 sprig thyme; a few mushroom trimmings; 1 glass port or claret; ½ pint Espagnole Sauce (p. 26); ¼ pint game stock; salt and pepper; 1 tbs. red-currant jelly.

Fry the finely chopped shallots golden in the oil, then add the bayleaf, thyme, mushroom trimmings and port or claret. Cover and cook for five minutes. Now add the Espagnole Sauce and game stock and simmer for ten minutes longer, skimming. Pass through a fine sieve, season with salt and pepper, and finish with red-currant jelly.

SAUCE À LA MOËLLE

This is made in the same way as a Sauce Bordelaise (p. 124) but white wine is used instead of red wine. It is garnished with dice of poached beef marrow and chopped fines herbes (parsley, chervil, chives and tarragon).

Serve with grilled meat, vegetables or poached eggs.

SAUCE ALBERT

1–2 tbs. Melted-Butter Sauce (p. 96); horseradish; cream; breadcrumbs; 1 egg yolk; dry mustard; vinegar.

This is a Melted-Butter Sauce flavoured to taste with grated horseradish and finished with cream. The breadcrumbs are then added, the sauce is brought to the boil and the whole rubbed through a sieve. It is then bound with the egg yolk, seasoned, and completed with a little mustard flour mixed with vinegar.

Use with poached fish.

SAUCE ALBUFÉRA

A Sauce Suprême (p. 152) finished with white meat glaze (p. 33) and Pimento Butter (p. 186).

Use with boiled chicken.

SAUCE À L'ESTRAGON 1

Thick veal gravy flavoured with tarragon essence and finished with chopped tarragon.

Use with boiled chicken.

SAUCE À L'ESTRAGON 2

A Velouté Sauce (p. 24) to which a little tarragon purée has been added, and finished with chopped tarragon.

Use as above.

SAUCE À L'HUILE

Grate the rinds of three lemons, and add them to four or five table-spoonfuls of olive oil, one or two mustardspoonfuls of mustard, the juice of the three lemons and a tablespoonful of vinegar. Stir until well mixed together.

Use as for vinaigrette.

SAUCE À L'HUILE PROVENÇALE

2 lemons; 2 tbs. oil; 1 tbs. vinegar; salt; garlic; parsley; tarragon; pepper.

Peel and slice the lemons thinly, and put the slices into a dish or sauce-boat with the oil, vinegar, salt, chopped garlic, parsley and tarragon and a little pepper. Mix well together to serve.

Use with grilled fish.

SAUCE ALLEMANDE

Basic sauce (see p. 25).

Use with boiled fish, chicken, veal and vegetables.

SAUCE AMIRAL

½ *pint Melted-Butter Sauce (p. 96); 2 anchovies; chives; capers; 1 lemon.*

Add to the Melted-Butter Sauce the well-pounded and sieved anchovies, some finely chopped chives and chopped capers. Simmer, with a few strips of thinly peeled lemon rind, over a gentle heat until well blended, then remove the peel, add the juice of the lemon and seasoning to taste, and serve.

Use with fish.

SAUCE ANCHOIS

See Anchovy Sauce (p. 41).

SAUCE ANDALOUSE

To half a pint of Mayonnaise Sauce (p. 28) add four tablespoonfuls of thick and very red tomato purée, and two small sweet red peppers cut in fine julienne strips.

Use as for Mayonnaise.

SAUCE APPÉTISSANTE

1 tsp. made mustard; 1 tsp. sugar; 2 tbs. Harvey's sauce; 1 tsp. chopped shallot; 1 tsp. chilli vinegar; 1 tbs. claret or port wine.

Work the sugar into the mustard, add the Harvey's sauce, shallot, chilli vinegar, and claret or port wine. French mustard may be added or other vinegars, or the proportion of each varied to taste. Put the whole in a silver dish over a lamp. Put in your slices of meat, or hot or cold game; let it cook till very hot. This is excellent, and will revive and stimulate the most jaded appetite.

Use with any meat and hot or cold game.

SAUCE AU BEURRE D'ANCHOIS

Colour a small piece of butter, and make a roux with a pinch of flour, letting this colour too. Then add, over a low heat, Anchovy Butter (p. 181) to your liking, finishing with a pinch of chopped tarragon. The sauce should be served immediately it is made.

Use with grilled meat.

SAUCE AU BEURRE DE L'AIL

Have ready a Velouté Sauce (p. 24), and, just before serving, whisk it quickly over heat without letting it boil, adding a little Garlic Butter (p. 183) and an equal quantity of fresh butter.

Use with meat.

SAUCE AU PORTO

Half-Glaze Sauce (p. 26) with a glass of port wine added at the last moment.

Use with mutton or game.

SAUCE AURORE 1

This is a Sauce Suprême (p. 152) lightly flavoured and coloured with tomato purée.

Use with meat.

SAUCE AURORE 2

Add four tablespoonfuls of very red and much reduced tomato purée to half a pint of Fish Velouté (p. 24) or White Wine Sauce (p. 179). Finish with two ounces of butter.

Use with fish.

SAUCE AURORE 3

Mix a tablespoonful of butter with a teaspoonful of paprika pepper and warm in a saucepan. Add a good pint of Béchamel Sauce (p. 24) enriched with cream. See that only the best, Hungarian paprika pepper (*edel süss*), is used here.

SAUCE AUX CERISES

6 tbs. white wine; 6 tbs. cherry juice; 4–5 tbs. stoned cherries; mixed spice; rind of 1 orange; 4–5 tbs. gooseberry jelly.

Put the white wine into a saucepan and add the cherry juice, a small pinch of mixed spice and the grated orange rind, and boil until reduced to half. Then add the gooseberry jelly and four or five tablespoonfuls of stoned ripe cherries and boil together for a few minutes. If red cherries are used, red-currant jelly can be used instead of gooseberry, which is more difficult to get.

Hand in a sauceboat with roast venison, roast or braised duck or goose.

SAUCE AUX HERBES

Finish a pint of White Wine Sauce (p. 179) with three ounces of Shallot Butter (p. 188), and a tablespoonful of parsley, chervil, tarragon and chives, chopped and mixed together.
See also Herb Sauce (p. 83).

Use with boiled fish.

SAUCE AUX HUÎTRES

See Oyster Sauce (p. 105).

SAUCE AUX NOIX

1 handful walnuts; olive oil; garlic; parsley.

Peel the walnuts and pound them well in a mortar. Fry in oil a very small quantity of garlic and parsley finely chopped together; add the walnut purée, cook a little but do not brown. Moisten with a little olive oil and very little boiling water. Mix well with hot spaghetti and serve immediately.

Use with spaghetti.

SAUCE AUX PIGNONS

1 pint Poivrade Sauce (p. 110); 2 oz. juniper berries; 1 oz. pine-kernels; 1 oz. raisins; $\frac{1}{8}$ pint Madeira.

Make a pint of ordinary Poivrade Sauce. Now prepare an infusion with the roughly-chopped juniper berries and a quarter of a pint of water. Grill the pine-kernels, and soak the stoned raisins in tepid water for about an hour. When the sauce is ready to be dished up, finish it by adding the finely strained infusion, the grilled pine-kernels, soaked raisins and Madeira.

Use with venison.

SAUCE BÂTARDE

3 oz. butter; 2 tbs. flour; 1 egg yolk; lemon juice; salt; pepper.

Melt one ounce of the butter and stir in the flour. Remove from heat and moisten with half a pint of boiling water. Beat well with a whisk. Add the egg yolk mixed with a tablespoonful of cold water. Season, add a few drops of lemon juice, and the rest of the butter.

Use with fish, poultry, vegetables.

SAUCE BÉARNAISE

1 tsp. chopped shallots; 2 oz. chopped tarragon stalks; 3 oz. chervil; mignonette pepper; salt; 4 tbs. vinegar; 5 egg yolks; 6 oz. melted butter; 1 tsp. chopped chervil and tarragon leaves; cayenne.

Put into a small stewpan the chopped shallots, tarragon stalks, chervil, some mignonette pepper, a pinch of salt and vinegar. Reduce the vinegar by two thirds, take off the heat, let the stewpan cool a little, and to this reduction add the egg yolks. Now put the stewpan on the lowest possible heat and gradually combine the melted butter with the yolks. Whisk the sauce briskly, so as to ensure the cooking of the yolks, which alone by gradual cooking effect the liaison of the sauce. It must never approach boiling or it will curdle. In fact it should always be kept at the lowest temperature consistent with cooking. When the butter has combined with the sauce, rub the latter through a tammy, and finish it with the chervil and tarragon leaves. Complete the seasoning with a suspicion of cayenne. This sauce should not be served very hot, as it is really a Mayonnaise with butter. It need only be tepid, for it would probably turn if it were overheated.

Use with grilled meat and poultry.

SAUCE BÉARNAISE WITH MEAT GLAZE

See Sauce Foyot (p. 131).

SAUCE BÉARNAISE TOMATÉE

Finish the Sauce Béarnaise described above with a third of a pint of very red tomato purée, and omit the final addition of chervil and tarragon.

Use with tournedos, grilled poultry, or fish.

SAUCE BELLE CRÉOLE

1 tbs. butter; 1 tbs. flour; 4 tbs. breadcrumbs; 8 tbs. consommé; 8 tbs. cream; salt and pepper; 1 tbs. chopped parsley; 1 tsp. onion juice; 2 hard-boiled egg yolks; lemon juice.

Make a white roux (p. 23) with the butter and flour, add the breadcrumbs, stir together and then moisten with the consommé. Stir well and add the cream, seasoning with salt and pepper. Then add the chopped parsley and onion juice, and when the sauce is smooth, take it off the heat and stir in the chopped egg yolks with a little lemon juice.

Use with boiled fish or boiled meat.

SAUCE BERCY

1 oz. chopped shallots; ¼ pint each white wine and fish fumet (p. 34); ⅙ pint Velouté Sauce (p. 24); 2 oz. butter; fish glaze (p. 35); ¼ lemon; ½ oz. parsley.

Heat the chopped shallots, and moisten them with the white wine and fish fumet. Reduce to a good third, then add the Velouté Sauce. Let the mixture boil for some time, then finish the sauce, away from the heat, with the butter added in little bits, a few drops of fish glaze, the juice of the lemon and chopped parsley.

Use with fish.

SAUCE BIGARADE

This sauce, which accompanies braised duckling as a rule, is described by Escoffier as follows: 'After having strained the braising sauce (of the duckling) completely, remove its grease, and reduce it until it is very dense. Strain it once more through muslin, twisting the latter; then, in order to bring the sauce to its normal consistency, add the juice of six oranges and one lemon per quart of sauce. Finish with a small piece of lemon and orange rind cut regularly and finely, julienne-fashion, and scalded for five minutes.'

Strain the stock through linen and return to the pan; entirely remove the grease, and add four pieces of caramel sugar dissolved in one tablespoonful of vinegar per one-half pint of stock, and the juice of the oranges and lemon and the julienne of rinds, as above. This sauce is also used with wild duck.

See also the recipes under Orange Sauce (pp. 103–105).

Use with braised duckling or wild duck.

SAUCE BOHÉMIENNE

2 dessertsp. Béchamel Sauce (p. 24); 2 egg yolks; salt and pepper; tarragon vinegar; about ¾ pint olive oil; tarragon.

Take the cold thick Béchamel Sauce, and mix with the egg yolks, salt, pepper and a few drops of tarragon vinegar. Then add the olive oil in the same manner as in making a Mayonnaise Sauce (p. 28), and finish it with a little finely chopped tarragon.

Use as for Mayonnaise.

SAUCE BONNE FEMME

1 oz. butter; 3 mushrooms; 1 onion; 1 carrot; 1 parsnip; 1 very small slice garlic; 2 sprigs parsley; 8 tbs. gravy; 8 tbs. white wine; salt and pepper; grated nutmeg; 1 handful breadcrumbs; ¼ pint milk.

Put the vegetables, garlic and parsley into a small saucepan with the butter. Moisten with the gravy and the white wine, season with salt, pepper and grated nutmeg, and boil gently for an hour. Then pass through a sieve. Boil the breadcrumbs in the milk until all the milk is absorbed; sieve this too, and then add it to the sauce, and heat through again together.

Use with poultry.

SAUCE BONNEFOY

See Sauce à la Moëlle (p. 116), but replace the Half-Glaze Sauce by Velouté Sauce (p. 24) and add chopped tarragon.

Use with lamb.

SAUCE BORDELAISE 1 (Blanche)

2 oz. minced shallots; ½ pint Graves, Sauternes or any other white Bordeaux wine; ¼ pint Velouté Sauce (p. 24); 6 oz. butter; tarragon.

Put the minced shallots and wine in a saucepan. Reduce the wine almost entirely, then add the Velouté Sauce, and rub it through a fine sieve. Finish, off the heat, with the butter and a little chopped tarragon.

Use with grilled fish or grilled white meat.

SAUCE BORDELAISE 2 (Rouge)

2 oz. finely minced shallots; ½ pint good red wine; mignonette pepper; thyme; bayleaf; ½ pint Half-Glaze Sauce (p. 26); 2 tbs. meat glaze (p. 33); lemon juice; 4 oz. beef marrow.

Put into a stewpan the very finely minced shallots, the wine, a pinch of mignonette pepper and bits of thyme and bay. Reduce the wine by three quarters, and add the Half-Glaze Sauce. Keep the sauce simmering for half an hour, skim it from time to time, and strain through linen or a sieve. When dishing it up, finish with the dissolved meat glaze, a few drops of lemon juice, and the beef marrow cut into slices or cubes and poached in slightly salted boiling water.

Use with grilled meat.

SAUCE BOURGUIGNONNE

3 oz. butter; 2 dessertsp. oil; 4 oz. mirepoix (p. 36); 1 pint red wine (Burgundy); salt and pepper; garlic; parsley; thyme; bayleaf; mushroom trimmings; brandy.

Fry without browning, in an ounce of butter and the oil, four ounces of a mirepoix composed of carrot, onion and celery. Drain off the fat, moisten with the red wine, add salt, pepper, a tiny bit of crushed garlic, a bouquet of parsley, thyme and bayleaf and some mushroom trimmings, and boil gently for twenty minutes. Pass it through a conical sieve, and bind it with kneaded butter. Finish with a couple of ounces of butter. A little brandy can be added, if liked.

Use with beef.

SAUCE BRETONNE 1

2 onions; butter; white wine; 2–3 fresh tomatoes; 1 tbs. tomato purée; garlic; parsley.

The chopped onions are fried golden in butter, then moistened with white wine, which is then reduced. The chopped tomatoes are then added, the tomato purée and a touch of garlic. When the sauce is cooked, it is sieved and thickened with kneaded butter. Roughly chopped parsley completes it.

Use with fish.

SAUCE BRETONNE 2

Julienne strips of leeks, celery, onions and mushrooms stewed in butter, are used to complete, as a garnish, a creamy and well-buttered fish Velouté Sauce (p. 24).

Use with fish.

SAUCE BRETONNE 3

2 tbs. finely chopped onion; 1 oz. butter; ½ pint dry white wine; ½ pint Espagnole Sauce (p. 26); ½ pint Tomato Sauce (p. 170); 1 clove garlic; parsley.

Fry the chopped onion in the butter until browned, then add the white wine and boil away until reduced by half. Now add the sauces, a crushed clove of garlic and a few sprigs of parsley. Boil for about ten minutes and strain through a sieve.

Used principally for haricot beans (haricots à la bretonne).

SAUCE BRUXELLOISE

Melt three ounces of fresh butter over a low heat and add salt, pepper and lemon juice to taste. Chop or sieve a hard-boiled egg finely, add this to the butter and serve when heated up.

Use with asparagus.

SAUCE CANOTIÈRE

fresh-water fish; court-bouillon (p. 34) with white wine; 4 oz. butter; 3 egg yolks; lemon juice.

Bind three quarters of a pint of stock, made from fresh water fish cooked in a court-bouillon with white wine, with two ounces of kneaded butter. Boil for a few minutes, then bind with three egg yolks. Finish with two ounces of butter and a few drops of lemon juice.

Use with fresh water fish.

SAUCE CARDINAL 1

1 pint Béchamel Sauce (p. 24); ½ pint fish fumet (p. 34); truffle essence; 3 tbs. cream; 3 oz. Lobster Butter (p. 184).

Boil the Béchamel Sauce, then add the fish fumet and a little truffle essence. Reduce this mixture by a quarter, and finish at the last with the cream and very red Lobster Butter.

Use with turbot, sole, lobster.

SAUCE CARDINAL 2

Add two or three ounces of Lobster Butter (p. 184) to each pint of Béchamel Sauce (p. 24) with cream, and season with a very little cayenne pepper, just enough to accentuate the flavour of the lobster.

Use as above.

SAUCE CHANTILLY 1

This hot sauce is simply Béchamel Sauce (p. 24) finished with two to three tablespoonfuls of whipped cream.

Use as for Mayonnaise.

SAUCE CHANTILLY 2

Mayonnaise Sauce (p. 28) made with lemon juice instead of vinegar, with two to three tablespoonfuls of whipped cream folded into it at the last minute before serving.

Use as for Mayonnaise.

SAUCE CHARCUTIÈRE

This is Sauce Robert (p. 149) garnished with chopped or diced pickled gherkins.

Use with pork.

SAUCE CHASSEUR

6 medium-sized mushrooms; ½ oz. butter; 1 tbs. olive oil; 1 tsp. minced shallots; ½ pint white wine; 4 tbs. brandy; ½ pint Half-Glaze Sauce (p. 26); ¼ pint Tomato Sauce (p. 170); 1 tbs. meat glaze (p. 33); 1 tsp. chopped parsley.

Peel and mince the mushrooms. Heat the butter and olive oil in a saucepan, put in the mushrooms and fry them quickly until they are slightly browned. Now add the minced shallots, and immediately pour off half the butter. Pour the white wine and brandy into the pan and reduce this liquid to half. Add the Half-Glaze Sauce, Tomato Sauce and meat glaze. Boil for five minutes or more, and finish with the parsley.

Use with lamb, beef, veal or chicken.

SAUCE CHATEAUBRIAND

1 oz. chopped shallots; 1 sprig thyme; ½ bayleaf; 1 oz. mushroom parings; ¾ pint white wine; ½ pint veal gravy (p. 36); 4 oz. Maître d'Hôtel Butter (p. 185); tarragon.

Put the chopped shallots, thyme and bayleaf into a saucepan with the mushroom parings and white wine. Reduce the wine almost entirely, then add the veal gravy, and reduce again until there is only a quarter of a pint of liquid. Strain through muslin, and finish, off the heat, with the Maître d'Hôtel Butter, to which may be added a little chopped tarragon.

Use with the fillet of beef known as a Chateaubriand.

SAUCE CHIVRY

½ *pint chicken stock (p. 33); a large pinch chervil, tarragon, chives and parsley; 1 head young burnet (pimprenelle); 1 pint Velouté Sauce (p. 24); 2 oz. Montpellier Butter (p. 185).*

Infuse the chervil, tarragon, parsley, burnet and chives in the boiling chicken stock, covered. After twelve minutes, strain the liquid through linen, and add it to the Velouté Sauce. Bring to the boil, reduce by a quarter, and finish with Montpellier Butter.

Use with boiled poultry.

SAUCE CHORON

This is a Sauce Béarnaise (p. 121) flavoured with tomato purée, one to two tablespoonfuls to taste.

Use with lamb cutlets.

SAUCE COLBERT

This is a light chicken glaze (p. 33) thickened with butter, and with chopped tarragon added to it.

Use with sole or chicken.

SAUCE CRÈME

½ *pint Béchamel Sauce (p. 24); ¼ pint fresh cream; lemon juice.*

Boil the Béchamel Sauce, adding half the fresh cream. Reduce until very thick, then pass it through a fine sieve. Now bring it back to its original consistency, by adding gradually, off the heat, the rest of the fresh cream and a few drops of lemon juice.

Use with any fish requiring a white sauce.

SAUCE CREVETTE NORMANDE

½ lb. shrimps; fish bones and trimmings; 1 onion; salt and pepper; few sprigs parsley; 1 tbs. butter; flour; lemon juice.

Boil the shrimps for half an hour with the fish bones and trimmings, onion, salt, pepper and parsley. Take off the heat, pound them and pass them through a fine sieve. Melt the butter in a saucepan, work in a little flour, and then mix in the shrimp purée, leaving it to cook for ten minutes on a slow heat. Squeeze in a little lemon juice before serving.

Use with fish.

SAUCE CURRY À LA CRÈME

This is the mild creamy curry sauce so much preferred by the French for domestic consumption to our own somewhat heartier version.

1½ oz. butter; 1 tbs. finely minced onion; 1 tsp. curry powder; ½ pint Béchamel Sauce (p. 24); 3–4 tbs. cream.

Brown the onion in the butter, then stir in the curry powder and cook for a few moments. Now add the Béchamel Sauce and simmer on a low heat for a few minutes. Rub through a fine sieve and lastly add the cream.

Particularly good for light fish dishes.

SAUCE DE LA VIELLE CHARLOTTE

hare; flour; vinegar; browned breadcrumbs.

Make sure in the first place that the hare is slightly underdone. Drain off the gravy and put back the hare to keep warm. In a small saucepan make a roux with flour and three tablespoonfuls of vinegar, and add to this the gravy from the hare. Pour this all into a sauceboat in which you have put about three quarters of a glassful of browned bread-crumbs – a version of bread sauce which will be welcomed for its savoury simplicity.

Use with roast Râble de Lièvre.

SAUCE DEMI-GLACE

See Half-Glaze Sauce (p. 26).

SAUCE DES HALLES

Mix some very finely chopped shallot with red wine vinegar, and season with coarsely crushed mignonette or black pepper. The amounts depend on how many oysters you are eating!

Use with oysters.

SAUCE DIABLE I

butter; 1 small onion; 2 shallots; 1 rasher bacon; bouquet of parsley, thyme and bayleaf; 1 tbs. vinegar; 1 tbs. tomato purée; 1 tbs. meat stock; salt and pepper; cayenne.

Fry lightly in a little butter the onion, shallots and bacon all chopped together, adding the bouquet of herbs and the vinegar. Let this boil until it is reduced by a quarter, and then add the tomato purée and meat stock and a seasoning of salt and pepper. Bring to the boil and simmer gently for five minutes, then add a pinch of cayenne, and strain and serve.

Use with beef, lamb or sometimes fish.

SAUCE DIABLE 2

4 shallots; butter; 6 mushrooms; 1 tbs. Harvey's sauce; 1 tbs. Worcestershire sauce; 1 tbs. mushroom ketchup; 4 tbs. good Brown Sauce (p. 26); a little chopped parsley, chervil and tarragon.

Stew the very finely chopped shallots in a little butter, and then add the finely chopped mushrooms. Cook for a few minutes longer and then stir in the Harvey's and Worcestershire sauce, mushroom ketchup, the Brown Sauce and chopped herbs. Simmer all together for about a quarter of an hour, then serve.

Use as above.

SAUCE DIANE

A Sauce Poivrade (p. 110) finished with cream to taste.

Use with game.

SAUCE ÉCOSSAISE I

A Sauce Normande (p. 143) garnished with little dice of carrots, truffles and celery.

Use with boiled fish or chicken.

SAUCE ÉCOSSAISE 2

A light Béchamel Sauce (p. 24) garnished with minced hard-boiled egg whites, and their yolks passed through a coarse sieve.

See also Egg Sauce (p. 71).

Use as above.

SAUCE ÉPICURIENNE

1 egg yolk; 2 tbs. cream; 1 pint fish Velouté (p. 24); 1 tbs. walnut ketchup; 1 tbs. chilli vinegar; butter; cayenne pepper.

Beat up the egg yolk in the cream, and add it to the fish Velouté; pass through a sieve, and heat it up with the walnut ketchup and the chilli vinegar. Finish with a small pat of butter kneaded with cayenne pepper.

Use with grilled fish.

SAUCE FOYOT

This is Sauce Béarnaise (p. 121) finished with a small piece of meat glaze (p. 33).

Serve with grilled or sautéed meat.

SAUCE GENEVOISE (English version)

2 oz. butter; 1 onion; 2 mushrooms; 1½ oz. flour; ¾ pint fish stock (p. 34); 1 small glass sherry or Madeira; ½ tsp. lemon juice; ½ tsp. anchovy essence; salt and pepper.

Melt the butter in a saucepan and fry the sliced onion until slightly browned. Add the sliced mushrooms, cook on a little, then sprinkle in the flour and cook until nut-brown. Now add the fish stock, the sherry or Madeira, lemon juice, anchovy essence, and salt and pepper to taste. Simmer gently for about twenty minutes, strain finely, and reheat to serve.

Use with fish.

SAUCE GODARD

½ pint white wine; 2 oz. mirepoix (p. 36); ham; Half-Glaze Sauce (p. 26); mushroom essence.

Make a reduction with the white wine and mirepoix and a little diced ham. Add this to a Half-Glaze Sauce flavoured with mushroom essence. Cook together for ten minutes only, and then sieve.

Use with beef or lamb.

SAUCE GRAND-VENEUR

½ pint Poivrade Sauce (p. 110); ½ pint game stock; 2 tbs. red-currant jelly; cream.

Boil up the Poivrade Sauce with the game stock, and let it reduce by a good third. Then take it off the heat, and add the red-currant jelly. Let this dissolve and then finish with a quarter of a pint of cream for each pint of the sauce.

Use with joints of venison.

SAUCE GRATIN

4 tbs. white wine; 4 tbs. fish fumet (p. 34); 1 dessertsp. chopped shallot; 4 dessertsp. duxelles (p. 35); 8 tbs. fish Velouté (p. 24); chopped parsley; butter.

Put the white wine and fish fumet into a saucepan with the chopped shallot, and reduce it by half. Add the duxelles and fish Velouté. Finish with butter and chopped parsley.

Use with fish.

SAUCE GRIBICHE

6 hard-boiled eggs; 1 tsp. French mustard; salt and pepper; oil; vinegar; gherkins; capers; chervil; tarragon; parsley.

Pound the egg yolks to a paste, add the French mustard, salt and pepper, and finish with oil and vinegar in the same manner as in making a Mayonnaise Sauce (p. 28). Finish the sauce by adding chopped gherkins, capers, chervil, tarragon and parsley, and several of the egg whites cut in thin julienne strips.

Use as for Mayonnaise.

SAUCE GRILLON

2 oz. butter; 1 tbs. flour; 2 tbs. cream; 1 tbs. milk; 1 tbs. mixed minced parsley and shallot; salt and pepper.

Make a white roux (p. 23) with the butter and flour, moisten first with the cream and then the milk, and stir over the heat until quite smooth. Then add the finely minced parsley and shallot, season with salt and pepper, and keep stirring over the heat until the sauce is quite hot but not boiling. It should look like thick cream.

Use with turbot, sole or whiting.

SAUCE HACHÉE I

1 onion; 2–3 shallots; butter; ¼ pint vinegar; ½ pint tomato-flavoured Half-Glaze Sauce (p. 26); ham; parsley; capers; duxelles (p. 35).

Chop the onions and shallots and stew them in butter without coloration. Moisten with the vinegar and reduce to half. Add tomato-flavoured Half-Glaze Sauce and boil for five minutes. Garnish with chopped ham and parsley, small capers and dry duxelles.

Use with meat.

SAUCE HACHÉE 2 (Maigre)

As above, but replace the Half-Glaze Sauce by fish Velouté (p. 24), and the ham by a few drops of anchovy essence. Finish with butter.

Use with fish.

SAUCE HOMARD

See Lobster Sauce 1 (p. 91).

SAUCE HONGROISE

onion; butter; paprika pepper; white wine; bouquet of parsley, thyme and bayleaf; Sauce Suprême (p. 152).

Lightly fry some chopped onion in butter and flavour with paprika pepper. Moisten with white wine and add the bouquet of herbs. Reduce by two thirds, and mix with Sauce Suprême.

See also Hungarian Sauce (p. 86).

Use with fish or veal.

SAUCE HUSSARDE I

1 onion; butter; 2–3 shallots; ¼ pint each white wine, tomato-flavoured Half-Glaze Sauce (p. 26) and white stock (p. 33); ham; garlic; parsley; thyme; bayleaf; horseradish.

Stew the minced onion in butter without coloration, add the minced shallots and moisten with white wine. Reduce this, and add tomato-flavoured Half-Glaze Sauce, a little white stock, some raw, lean ham, a touch of garlic, and a bouquet of parsley, thyme and bayleaf. Cook for twenty-five minutes and then rub through a sieve after taking out the ham. Cut this into small dice and add them to the sauce with grated horseradish and chopped parsley.

Use with meat.

SAUCE HUSSARDE 2

1 onion; ½ clove garlic; 1 bayleaf; 2 oz. chopped ham; ½ pint mixed white wine and stock; pepper; parsley; tarragon; shallot; celery root; butter; flour; meat extract.

Cut the onion in slices, and fry it lightly with the garlic, bayleaf and chopped ham. Then moisten it with white wine and stock and season with pepper, parsley, tarragon, shallot and celery root. Bring to the boil, and when the sauce is cooked, bind it with butter and flour, add a little meat extract if you like, and sieve before serving.

Use with meat.

SAUCE INDIENNE

1 tbs. curry powder or paste; butter; ½ pint Sauce Allemande (p. 25) or Sauce Espagnole (p. 26); lemon juice; cayenne.

Fry the curry powder or paste in a little butter for a few minutes, let it get cold and then knead it with some fresh butter. Add an ounce or so of this butter to half a pint of Sauce Allemande (for a light sauce) or of Espagnole (if it is to be dark), and finish with a dash of lemon juice and a little cayenne pepper.

Use with fish, eggs, white meat.

SAUCE INFERNALE

1 wild duck; 3 sprigs parsley; 1 lemon; 1 shallot; liver of duck; 6 tbs. good red wine; salt; made mustard.

Roast the duck, a little underdone, and meanwhile chop up some parsley, lemon rind and shallot in nearly equal proportions. Add the chopped cooked liver of the duck, the drippings in the pan, the red wine, salt, a little made mustard and the juice of the lemon. Mix all well together and serve.

Use with wild duck.

SAUCE ITALIENNE I

3 tbs. duxelles (p. 35); 1 oz. lean ham; ½ pint Half-Glaze Sauce with tomato (p. 26); parsley; chervil; tarragon.

Put into a saucepan the duxelles, the lean cooked ham cut very fine, and the Half-Glaze Sauce with tomato. After boiling for ten minutes, finish the sauce at the last minute with half a teaspoonful of parsley, chervil and tarragon, minced and mixed.

Use with beef or mutton.

SAUCE ITALIENNE 2

The cold sauce of this name is a Mayonnaise Sauce (p. 28) finished with a purée of cooked calf's brains and chopped fines herbes (parsley, chervil, chives and tarragon).

Use as for Mayonnaise in salad.

SAUCE ITALIENNE 3

Put three quarters of a pint of Half-Glaze Sauce with tomato (p. 26) into a pan, with two tablespoonfuls of finely chopped mushrooms and the same weight of shredded cooked streaky bacon. Boil together for five minutes and then add a pinch of chopped parsley.

SAUCE IVOIRE

This is a Sauce Suprême (p. 152) finished with white meat glaze (p. 33).

Use with poultry and veal.

SAUCE JOINVILLE 1

A White Wine Sauce (p. 179) finished with a purée of shrimps or prawns and garnished with small shrimps.

Use with fish.

SAUCE JOINVILLE 2

A Sauce Normande (p. 143) finished with a purée of shrimps or prawns, which may be garnished with a julienne of truffles.

Use as above.

SAUCE JOINVILLE 3

Bind half a pint of creamy Béchamel Sauce (p. 24) with two egg yolks beaten in two or three tablespoonfuls of cream and finished with an ounce of Lobster Butter (p. 184) and a squeeze of lemon juice.

Use as above.

SAUCE LAGUIPIERRE

Sauce Bâtarde (p. 121) finished with fish glaze (p. 35).

Use with fish.

SAUCE LANDAISE

2 sweet red peppers; olive oil; 2–3 tomatoes; bouquet of parsley, thyme, bayleaf and 1 rosemary leaf; 2 finely chopped gherkins; 1 tbs. vinegar.

Cut the red peppers into slices, remove the pips, and cook them in olive oil for a few minutes. Then add the tomatoes, less their skin and pips, also cut in small pieces, and the bouquet of herbs. Cook on slowly until the mixture is almost a pulp, then add the gherkins and vinegar. Take out the bouquet, and cook for two or three minutes longer.

Use with meat or boiled fish.

SAUCE LIVONIENNE

This is a rich fish Velouté (p. 24) garnished with a julienne of truffles, carrots and chopped parsley.

Use with fish.

SAUCE LIVORNAISE

See Leghorn Sauce (p. 89).

SAUCE LYONNAISE 1

2 oz. finely minced onions; 2 oz. butter; ¼ pint white wine; ¼ pint vinegar; 1½ pints clear Half-Glaze Sauce (p. 26).

Brown the onions slightly in the butter, then moisten with the wine and vinegar. Reduce this almost completely and then add the Half-Glaze Sauce, and cook slowly for half an hour. The onion may be left in the sauce, or the sauce strained, according to the taste of the diners.

Use with white meat.

SAUCE LYONNAISE 2 (Créole)

Make a Tomato Sauce (p. 170) and add to this some well-minced onions first browned in butter and a little lemon juice as well.

Use with white meat.

SAUCE MADÈRE (Madeira Sauce)

1½ pints Half-Glaze Sauce (p. 26); ⅕ pint Madeira.

Reduce the Half-Glaze Sauce until it is stiff, then remove it from the heat and add the Madeira, which should bring it back to its original consistency. Strain through a fine sieve and keep it warm without allowing it to boil, but not for too long, or the flavour of the wine will be dissipated.

Use with ham etc.

SAUCE MALTAISE

This is a Hollandaise Sauce (p. 27) to which is added a little blood-orange juice with a julienne of some of the blanched rind.

Use with asparagus.

SAUCE MARGUÉRY

This is a Hollandaise Sauce (p. 27) flavoured with a tablespoon of fish fumet (p. 34) and a tablespoon of oyster purée.

Use with fish.

SAUCE MARINIÈRE 1

A Sauce Bercy (p. 122) to which a tablespoon of strong reduced mussel cooking liquor has been added. It is garnished with small poached and bearded mussels.

Use with fish.

SAUCE MARINIÈRE 2

A Sauce Poulette (p. 146) with a very little finely chopped shallot and some chopped parsley added to it.

Use with fish.

SAUCE MARQUISE

1 handful breadcrumbs; butter; 1 tbs. olive oil; 1 shallot; salt; whole pepper; vinegar.

Take the chopped breadcrumbs, a pat of butter the size of a half-crown, the olive oil, the shallot minced fine, some salt, whole pepper and put all this into a saucepan. Place over heat with enough vinegar to cover, and stir with a wooden spoon until it boils. Then sieve and serve.

Use with fish or lamb.

SAUCE MATELOTE 1 (Blanche)

fish court-bouillon; white wine; mushrooms; fish Velouté (p. 24); cayenne; butter; button onions.

A reduction of a strained fish court-bouillon with white wine and mushroom trimmings is added to fish Velouté, sieved, seasoned with a little cayenne pepper and finished with butter. The fish which this sauce accompanies is garnished with small white mushrooms and white glazed button onions.

The richer the fish, the richer the sauce should be.

SAUCE MATELOTE 2 (Rouge)

salmon head; maigre mirepoix (p. 36); butter; brandy; red wine; celery; garlic; mushrooms; salt; thyme; bayleaf; button onions; croûtons of fried bread.

Fry a chopped-up salmon head and a maigre mirepoix in butter without coloration. This is flambéed with brandy, moistened with red wine, and the following ingredients are added; a piece of celery, crushed garlic, mushroom trimmings, salt, coarsely ground pepper, thyme and a bayleaf. This is all boiled until reduced by half, then strained, bound with kneaded butter and finished with fresh butter. The fish which this sauce accompanies is always garnished with button mushrooms, glazed button onions and heart-shaped croûtons of bread fried in butter.

Use with fish as above.

SAUCE MAYONNAISE ESCOFFIER

This is a Mayonnaise Sauce (p. 28) to which have been added grated horseradish, and chopped chervil and parsley to taste.

Use as for Mayonnaise.

SAUCE MESSINE

2 tbs. mixed chopped chervil, parsley, tarragon, shallot and lemon peel;
½ pint fresh cream; butter; flour; 2 egg yolks; 1 tbs. made mustard; juice
of 1 lemon.

Put the finely chopped chervil, parsley, tarragon, shallot and a little
lemon peel into a saucepan, just before you want the sauce, with the
cream, a little butter kneaded with flour, the raw egg yolks and made
mustard. Stir them together continuously until the cream is just
coming to the boil (but it must not actually boil), and then stir in
the lemon juice. This sauce must not be put on the heat until just
before it is wanted.

Use with fish.

SAUCE MONTGLAS

½ tbs. flour; butter; mushroom liquor; 2–3 egg yolks; milk; lemon juice;
truffle; parsley; shrimps.

Knead half a tablespoonful of flour with fresh butter and moisten it
with mushroom liquor. Boil together for ten minutes, then add to it,
off the heat, the egg yolks beaten with a little milk. Put the sauce back
on the fire until it just comes to the boil, stirring all the time. The
sauce should then be thick. Dilute it with a little lemon juice and add
very thin strips of truffle, chopped parsley and shrimps.

Use with fish.

SAUCE MORNAY

Béchamel Sauce (p. 24); fumet of fish, poultry or vegetable (p. 34)
Gruyère; Parmesan; butter.

This delicious sauce is usually travestied by some simpler kind of
cheese sauce, but it is worth while reading what Escoffier writes about
it in order to taste it at its very best. 'Boil,' he says, 'one pint of
Béchamel Sauce with one quarter-pint of the fumet of the fish,
poultry or vegetable, which is to constitute the dish. Reduce by a
good quarter, and add two ounces of Gruyère and two ounces of
grated Parmesan. Put the sauce on the heat again for a few minutes,

and ensure the melting of the cheese by stirring with a small whisk. Finish the sauce away from the heat with two ounces of butter added by degrees.'

Use with fish, eggs, vegetables.

SAUCE MOUSQUETAIRE

A Mayonnaise Sauce (p. 28) with two to three chopped shallots cooked in white wine. It is finished with a little cayenne pepper and chopped chives.

Use as for Mayonnaise.

SAUCE MOUSSELINE

This is a Hollandaise Sauce (p. 27) to which has been added, in a double saucepan, an equal quantity of stiffly whipped double cream. This should be done very gently, whipping carefully all the time. The seasoning will have to be slightly corrected.

Use with fish as for Hollandaise.

SAUCE MOUSSELINE DIJONNAISE

3 egg yolks; juice of 1 lemon; salt; white pepper; butter; 1 tbs. Dijon mustard.

Put into a saucepan the egg yolks, the lemon juice, a teaspoonful of cold water, salt, a pinch of white pepper and according to the amount of sauce you want, some dice of fresh cold butter. Put the pan into a larger one containing boiling water and whisk the contents until light and frothy. It is then ready, and all you have to do is to add the Dijon mustard and correct the seasoning.

Use with boiled or grilled fish, and for eggs fried in the French fashion or œufs mollets.

SAUCE MOUSSEUSE

4 oz. butter; 3 oz. flour; salt; lemon juice; 2 tbs. stiffly whipped cream.

Rinse a bowl in very hot water and wipe dry. Soften the butter to a creamy consistency and put into the bowl. Smoothly combine with the flour, a little salt and a few drops of lemon juice. Whisk into it by degrees a sixth of a pint of cold water. When mixed, finish with the whipped cream. Serve cold.

Use with boiled fish or vegetables.

SAUCE NANTAISE

white roux (p. 23); stock; 2 shallots; 2 pickled gherkins; 1 tbs. vinegar; 2 egg yolks; 1 tsp. Dijon mustard.

Make a white roux, and moisten it with a little stock. Add the chopped shallots, the gherkins finely minced and the vinegar. Then moisten with more stock to your requirements, and cook for half an hour. Mix together in a separate basin the egg yolks and the Dijon mustard. When the sauce is ready, bind it with this mixture without letting it boil again.

Use with fresh pork.

SAUCE NANTUA

½ pint Béchamel Sauce (p. 24); just over ¼ pint cream; 1½ oz. Crayfish Butter (p. 183); 1 dessertsp. small crayfish tails.

Boil the Béchamel Sauce, adding a quarter of a pint of cream, and reducing it by a third. Rub through a fine sieve, and finish it with a tablespoonful of cream, the Crayfish Butter and crayfish tails, cooked and shelled.

Use with fish.

SAUCE NEWBURG

1 lobster; butter; salt; cayenne pepper; sherry; 2 egg yolks; ⅓ pint fresh cream.

In order to make a Sauce Newburg, we shall have to cook a lobster *à la Newburg*, and as we are somewhat squeamish as a race in these matters, we shall make it from a cooked lobster, though with live lobster it is better. Take the meat from the tail shell and cut it in slices. Butter a stewpan generously, and arrange these slices on the bottom.

Season them highly with salt and cayenne pepper, and fry the pieces lightly on each side, without browning which will redden their skin. Then cover with good sherry, and cook until it is almost completely reduced. Just before serving, pour the egg yolks beaten up in the cream, over the slices and gently stir and roll the pan about on the lowest of low heats until the sauce is thickened. If this sauce is used with sole or other suitable fish, the pieces of lobster may be used as a garnish. Variations can be achieved by the addition of paprika pepper or of curry powder.

Use with sole, lobster and other shellfish.

SAUCE NIÇOISE

This is a Mayonnaise Sauce (p. 28) to which is added a quarter of its volume of much reduced tomato purée, one tablespoon of pounded sweet red peppers, and chopped tarragon.

Use as for Mayonnaise.

SAUCE NOISETTE

This is a Hollandaise Sauce (p. 27) made with Noisette Butter (p. 186) in place of fresh butter.

Use as for Hollandaise.

SAUCE NORMANDE I

butter; trimmings of fish; 1 onion; a bouquet of parsley, thyme and bayleaf; salt and pepper; ½ pint cider or white wine; 1½ oz. flour; 2 egg yolks; ¼ pint cream; lemon juice.

Stew in a little butter the trimmings of your fish with a minced onion, the bouquet of herbs and a seasoning of salt and pepper moistening with the cider or white wine. Strain. Make a white roux with one and a half ounces of butter and the flour. Add the liquid, whisk well and bring to the boil. Boil, stirring, for one minute. Blend yolks and cream. Add drops of hot sauce, beating well, then gradually pour in the sauce as a thin stream. Return to pan and bring to the boil, stirring well. Boil for a minute or two. Finish with a squeeze of lemon, and pass it through a sieve or muslin cloth over the fish.

Use with fish, eggs, vegetables.

SAUCE NORMANDE 2

1 onion; butter; flour; ½ pint cider or white wine; salt and pepper; nutmeg or cinnamon; cream; lemon juice.

Fry the finely minced onion lightly in a large nut of butter, add a little more butter, sprinkle with flour, mix in, and moisten with cider or white wine, whipping all the time with a whisk, and adding a few more little bits of butter. Season with salt, pepper and either grated nutmeg or ground cinnamon, and just before serving add about four tablespoonfuls fresh cream and finish with a touch of lemon juice. Strain.

Use with meat and vegetables.

SAUCE PALOISE

Sauce Béarnaise (p. 121) in which mint is used in place of tarragon.

Use with grilled cutlets.

SAUCE PARISIENNE

Basic sauce (see p. 25).

Use with meat.

SAUCE PÉRIGUEUX

Reduce until as thick as possible half a pint of Half-Glaze Sauce (p. 26) and then add a tablespoonful of chopped peeled truffles and finally a couple of tablespoonfuls of Madeira. This is a very rich sauce.

Use with fillet of beef, fresh foie-gras, vol-au-vents or timbales.

SAUCE PÉRIGOURDINE

This is a Half-Glaze Sauce (p. 26) enriched with a purée of foie-gras to taste. It is garnished with small dice of truffles.

Use with chicken and meat.

Savoury Sauces

SAUCE PETIT-MAÎTRE

1 glass white wine; ½ lemon; bread; 2 tsp. salad oil; 1 bunch parsley; 2–3 small onions; 2 cloves; tarragon; salt and pepper; 1¼ pint good stock.

Put into a saucepan the white wine, half a lemon cut in slices, a piece of bread without the crust chopped small, the salad oil, parsley, onions, cloves, a few leaves of tarragon, a little salt and pepper and the stock. Set on a gentle heat and boil for a quarter of an hour. Then skim off the grease, strain through a sieve and serve.

Use with poultry or game.

SAUCE PIMPRENELLE

1 tbs. cream; 1 tbs. vinegar; 1–2 tbs. oil; 1 egg yolk; salt and pepper; 2–3 tbs. chopped burnet.

The herb with which this attractive sauce is flavoured is not the Pimpernel, but Burnet. The sauce is sometimes found in Lorraine, where it is served with boiled beef, the garnish of carrot and turnip then being omitted. It is very simply made by adding to a good tablespoon of double cream the vinegar, oil, raw egg yolk, salt and pepper and finely chopped burnet. They are all mixed well together and that is all.

Use with boiled fresh beef.

SAUCE PIQUANTE

2 oz. minced shallots; ¼ pint white wine; ¼ pint vinegar; 1 pint Half-Glaze Sauce (p. 26); 2 oz. gherkins; 2 oz. capers; 1 tsp. mixed parsley, chervil and tarragon.

Put the minced shallots, white wine and vinegar into a saucepan. Reduce by a good half, and then add the Half-Glaze Sauce. Bring to the boil and reduce gently for half an hour. Finish at the last with gherkins, capers and the mixed herbs, all finely chopped.

Use with beef and lamb.

SAUCE PORTUGAISE

½ *lb. onions; olive oil; 3 tomatoes; salt; black pepper; Tomato Sauce* *(p. 170); meat glaze (p. 33); garlic; parsley.*

Stew the chopped onions in olive oil, and add roughly chopped tomatoes, salt, freshly ground black pepper, a little thin Tomato Sauce to adjust the thickness, a small piece of melted meat glaze, a touch of garlic and some chopped parsley. Cook all to a purée, and sieve.

Use with meat.

SAUCE POULETTE

Boil for a few minutes a pint of Sauce Allemande (p. 25), and add six tablespoonfuls of mushroom liquor. Finish off the heat with two ounces of butter in little pieces, a few drops of lemon juice, and a teaspoonful of chopped parsley.

Use with fish, poultry, white meat and vegetables.

SAUCE PROVENÇALE I

olive oil; ½ lb. tomatoes; salt; black pepper; sugar; 1 small clove garlic; *parsley.*

Heat a little olive oil in a saucepan until it smokes, then add the peeled and roughly chopped tomatoes, salt, freshly ground black pepper, a pinch of sugar, the garlic and chopped parsley. Cook for twenty minutes only.

Use with beef or lamb.

SAUCE PROVENÇALE 2

Add to the above some minced mushrooms fried in oil, and finish with thin Tomato Sauce (p. 170).

Use as above.

SAUCE PROVENÇALE 3

2 egg yolks; 2 tbs. Allemande Sauce (p. 25); a little pounded garlic; *powdered chillis; juice of 2 lemons; olive oil.*

Put into a small saucepan the egg yolks with the Allemande Sauce, garlic, a pinch of powdered chillis and lemon juice. Cook slowly in a bain-marie (or another saucepan containing boiling water) until the sauce has a little body, then take it from the heat and add little by little enough olive oil to give it the right consistency, stirring all the time. It can be finished with chopped parsley.

Use, hot, for chicken or fish entrées.

SAUCE PROVENÇALE FROIDE

2 cloves garlic; 3 salted anchovy fillets; 2 egg yolks; nearly ½ pint olive oil; lemon juice.

Pound in a mortar very finely the garlic, and anchovy fillets, add the egg yolks, a tablespoonful of cold water and a little salt, then stir in by degrees nearly half a pint of olive oil. Finish with lemon juice.

Use as for Mayonnaise.

SAUCE RAITO

4 tbs. olive oil; 2 large onions; 1 tbs. flour; 1 litre red wine; salt and pepper; 3 large tomatoes; 2 cloves; 3 cloves garlic; 3–4 pounded nuts, preferably walnuts; a bouquet of 2 bayleaves, 1 sprig thyme, rosemary and fennel and a good sprig of parsley; 1 tbs. each of capers and black olives.

A highly flavoured sauce of Greek origin. Heat the olive oil, and add one large chopped onion. When this has coloured, add the flour, stir well, and when it has coloured too, moisten it, little by little, with the red wine and half a litre of boiling water, adding salt, pepper, the tomatoes quartered, a large onion stuck with two cloves, the garlic, nuts and bouquet of herbs. Boil gently until it is reduced by two thirds. Then pass it through a sieve and add the capers and black olives.

Use with meat.

SAUCE RAVIGOTE I (Hot)

Mix a quarter of a pint of white wine with half as much vinegar, and reduce by half. Add a pint of Velouté Sauce (p. 24), and after boiling

for a few minutes, finish with an ounce and a half of Shallot Butter
(p. 188) and one teaspoonful of chervil, tarragon and chopped chives.

Use with calf's head.

SAUCE RAVIGOTE 2 (Cold)

This is simply a mixture of five parts olive oil, two parts vinegar, a
little French mustard, very finely chopped onion washed and pressed
dry, chopped parsley, chervil, tarragon and salt and pepper.

Use with calf's head.

SAUCE REFORM

*1 pint Half-Glaze Sauce (p. 26); ½ pint Poivrade Sauce (p. 110); ½ oz.
gherkins; ½ oz. hard-boiled egg white; 1 oz. tongue; 1 oz. truffles; 1 oz.
mushrooms.*

Combine the Half-Glaze Sauce with the Poivrade Sauce and heat
gently. Complete with a garnish of julienne strips of the gherkins,
hard-boiled egg white, tongue, truffles and mushrooms. This is the
sauce that accompanies Soyer's famous creation *Cutlets à la Reform*,
which he composed when he was chef to the Reform Club.

SAUCE RÉGENCE 1

This is a Sauce Normande (p. 143) to which have been added the
reduced cooking liquor of mushrooms and a little essence of truffles.

Use with fish.

SAUCE RÉGENCE 2

The same additions are made to a Sauce Suprême (p. 152) instead of a
Sauce Normande.

Use with meat.

SAUCE RÉMOULADE

To three quarters of a pint of Mayonnaise Sauce (p. 28) add a good
dessertspoonful of French mustard, and two dessertspoonfuls of

mixed chopped gherkin, capers, parsley, chervil and tarragon. Finish with a few drops of anchovy essence.

Use as for Mayonnaise.

SAUCE ROBERT

1 medium-sized onion; butter; $\frac{1}{6}$ pint white wine; $\frac{1}{2}$ pint Half-Glaze Sauce (p. 26); 1 dessertsp. meat glaze (p. 33); $\frac{1}{2}$ tsp. made mustard; castor sugar.

Mince the onion finely and fry it with a little butter without letting it colour. Now dilute it with the white wine and reduce this by a third. Add the Half-Glaze Sauce and simmer for twenty minutes. When the sauce is ready, finish it with the meat glaze, made mustard and a small pinch of castor sugar.

Use with beef, lamb or pork.

SAUCE ROUENNAISE 1

This is a Sauce Bordelaise (p. 124) with which have been mixed four raw duck livers sieved to a fine purée for each pint of the sauce. When they are added to the sauce, it must be heated for a few minutes so that the livers poach in it, but care must be taken not to heat the sauce too much or for too long, or the liver will be overcooked.

Use with Caneton Rouennaise.

SAUCE ROUENNAISE 2

1 onion; 3 fl. oz. cider or red wine; 3 tbs. meat glaze (p. 33); 3 tbs. gravy; salt; black pepper or cayenne; lemon juice.

Brown the onion cut into small dice and moisten this with the cider or red wine. Reduce it completely and then add the meat glaze, gravy, salt, freshly-ground black pepper or cayenne and a dash of lemon juice. Reduce again and strain before pouring over the meat.

Use with roast duck.

SAUCE RUSSE

See Russian Sauce (p 115).

SAUCE SAINT-MALO

This is a White Wine Sauce (p. 179) flavoured with made mustard, a drop of anchovy essence and chopped shallots cooked in white wine.

Use with fish.

SAUCE SAUPIQUET

white roux (p. 23); gravy or veal stock (p. 32), and a little white wine ($\frac{1}{2}$ pint in all); 2–3 shallots; a few peppercorns; 3 fl. oz. vinegar; cream; butter; tarragon.

Make a white roux, and moisten it with the gravy, veal stock and white wine. In a separate saucepan put the chopped shallots and crushed peppercorns, pour over the vinegar, and let it reduce. Add this to the first sauce, simmer for ten minutes and pass through a conical sieve. It should be thick enough to allow you to add a quarter of its volume of cream, and then you have only to finish it with a good piece of fresh butter and some chopped tarragon.

Use with poultry.

SAUCE SMITANE (Sour Cream Sauce)

1 tbs. finely chopped onion; $\frac{1}{2}$ oz. butter; $\frac{1}{4}$ pint dry white wine; 1 pint sour or soured cream; juice of $\frac{1}{4}$ lemon.

Brown the onion in the butter, then add the white wine and let it reduce almost entirely. Now add the cream and boil for a few minutes to thicken slightly. Strain through a sieve and finally squeeze in the lemon juice.

SAUCE SOLFÉRINO

This sauce is composed of meat glaze (p. 33) thickened with a mixture of Shallot and Maître d'Hôtel Butters (pp. 188 and 185), and finished with essence of tomatoes, lemon juice and a touch of cayenne pepper.

Use with meat.

SAUCE SOUBISE

2 lb. onions; butter; ½ pint thick Béchamel Sauce (p. 24); salt; 1 tsp. castor sugar; cream.

Scald the finely minced onion for three minutes, drain and dry, and stew in butter.

Add the Béchamel Sauce and season with salt and the castor sugar. Cook gently for half an hour, then rub through a fine sieve and finish with two ounces of butter and some cream.

Use with anything that goes with onion.

SAUCE SOUBISE TOMATÉE

To the above finished sauce, add a third of its volume of tomato purée.

Use as above.

SAUCE SUCHET OR SOUCHET

4 oz. mixed carrot, leek and celery; butter; fish fumet (p. 34); ¾ pint White Wine Sauce (p. 179).

Cut up equal portions of the red part of a carrot and the white of leeks and celery into fine julienne strips, so that there are four ounces in all. Stew these in butter and finish their cooking with a little light fish fumet. When they are cooked, reduce the liquid completely and mix the julienne with the White Wine Sauce.

Use with boiled fish.

SAUCE SUÉDOISE

A purée of about a pound of apples cooked in a little white wine is mixed with Mayonnaise Sauce (p. 28) and finished with grated horseradish.

Use with lamb cutlets.

SAUCE SUPRÊME (Velouté with Cream)

1½ pints clear chicken stock (p. 33); ¼ pint mushroom cooking liquor (p. 37); 1 pint chicken Velouté (p. 24); just over ½ pint cream; butter.

Put the chicken stock into a saucepan with the mushroom cooking liquor, and reduce to two thirds. Add the chicken Velouté, stirring all the while, and continue to reduce. When the sauce has reduced by a third again, add the cream, still stirring all the time. When the sauce coats the spoon strain through a sieve, and enrich with more cream and butter.

Use with roast chicken.

SAUCE TARTARE

A Mayonnaise Sauce (p. 28) made with hard-boiled egg yolk, garnished with finely chopped onions and chives and highly seasoned.

SAUCE TORTUE

½ pint veal stock (p. 33); 1 small sprig sage, sweet marjoram, rosemary, basil, thyme; 1 bayleaf; 2 oz. mushroom parings; 1 oz. parsley; 4 peppercorns; ½ pint Half-Glaze Sauce (p. 26); ½ pint Tomato Sauce (p. 170); 4 tbs. sherry; truffle essence; cayenne.

Boil the veal stock, adding the herbs, mushroom parings and parsley. Cover and infuse for half an hour. Two minutes before straining the infusion, add four roughly crushed peppercorns. After straining through fine linen, add the Half-Glaze Sauce and Tomato Sauce off the heat, with sherry, a little truffle essence and a good pinch of cayenne. As this sauce must be spicy the use of cayenne suggests itself, but great caution should be observed as there must be no excess of this condiment.

Use with calf's head.

SAUCE TYROLIENNE 1

This is a Sauce Choron (p. 128) in the making of which oil is used instead of butter.

Use with fish.

SAUCE TYROLIENNE 2

¾ pint clear fish stock (p. 34); 6 fl. oz. sherry; 1 oz. glaze; 1 shallot; 1 bayleaf; thyme; parsley; black pepper; ¼ pint tomato pulp; 1 oz. cornflour; truffles; cream or butter.

Boil together the fish stock, sherry, glaze, minced shallot, bayleaf, a bouquet of thyme and parsley, and a pinch of black pepper. Simmer gently for ten minutes, then strain on to the tomato pulp, which you have previously rubbed smooth with cornflour. Stir over the heat until it boils again, then sieve and finish with sliced truffles and a pat of butter or a spoonful of cream.

Use with fish.

SAUCE TYROLIENNE 3

Add to six fl. ounces of Mayonnaise Sauce (p. 28) a level teaspoonful and a half of capers, three dessertspoonfuls of tomato purée, a level teaspoonful and a half of finely chopped parsley and one finely chopped pickled gherkin.

Use with fish.

SAUCE VALOIS

See Sauce Foyot (p. 131).

SAUCE VERON

Three parts Sauce Tyrolienne 1 (p. 153) and one part Sauce Normande (p. 143) are blended together. Finish with a little dissolved light meat glaze (p. 33) and anchovy essence.

Use with fish.

SAUCE VERTE

See Green Sauce (p. 80).

SAUCE VICTORIA

This is a White Wine Sauce (p. 179) made with fish Velouté (p. 24), and finished with Shrimp or Lobster Butter (pp. 188 and 184). In the special dish *Sole Victoria*, only Lobster Butter should be used.

Use with lobster, sole or turbot.

SAUCE VILLAGEOISE

This is an ordinary Velouté Sauce (p. 24) flavoured with onion. It is then diluted with veal gravy and mushroom liquor, bound with egg yolk and cream, and finished with butter.

Use with veal or chicken.

SAUCE VILLEROY I

Reduce a pint of Sauce Allemande (p. 25), to which you have added two tablespoonfuls each of truffle essence and ham essence, until it is thick and stiff enough for the coating purposes for which this sauce is used.

Use to coat fish, meat or vegetables for frying.

SAUCE VILLEROY 2

Reduce a Sauce Parisienne (p. 25) until it is thick enough to use as a preliminary coating for certain food before breadcrumbing them and frying them in deep fat or oil.

Use as above.

SAUCE VILLEROY TOMATÉE

Add to the above sauce a third of its volume of tomato purée and reduce in the same way.

Use as above.

SAUCE VILLEROY SOUBISÉE

This is a mixture of two thirds Sauce Allemande (p. 25) and one-third Sauce Soubise (p. 151) reduced as above.

Use as above.

SAUCE VINCENT 1

herbs as for Green Sauce (p. 80); 20 sorrel leaves; 3 hard-boiled egg yolks; 2 raw egg yolks; oil; vinegar; salt and pepper.

Take the same herbs as for Green Sauce and add the sorrel. Blanch them, plunge them into cold water, drain and dry and pound them as directed before, but add when pounding the hard-boiled egg yolks. Pass through a fine sieve, add the raw egg yolks, and use this as a basis for a Mayonnaise Sauce (p. 28), adding oil and vinegar in the usual way. Season with salt and pepper.

Use as for Mayonnaise.

SAUCE VINCENT 2

A half-and-half mixture of Sauce Tartare (p. 152) and Green Sauce (p. 80).

Use as for Mayonnaise.

SAUCE VIN BLANC

See White Wine Sauce (p. 179).

Use with fish.

SAUCE VIN ROUGE

3 shallots; ½ pint red wine; 1 tbs. fish glaze (p. 35); butter; anchovy essence; cayenne.

A reduction is made with chopped shallots and red wine, fish glaze is added and the sauce is thickened with butter. It is finished with several drops of anchovy essence and a touch of cayenne pepper.

Use with fish e.g. salmon.

SAUCE ZINGARA I

This is a tomato-flavoured Half-Glaze Sauce (p. 26), garnished with a julienne of mushrooms, truffles, ham and tongue. A little cayenne pepper is added, and a few drops of Madeira at the very end.

Use with veal, chicken or lamb.

SAUCE ZINGARA 2

4 shallots; ¼ pint vinegar; ½ pint brown gravy; 2 tbs. fried breadcrumbs; parsley; lemon juice.

The chopped shallots are moistened with the vinegar, which is then reduced. The brown gravy is added and the thickening of fried breadcrumbs. After five minutes cooking the sauce is finished with chopped parsley and a dash of lemon juice.

Use as above.

SAUCE FOR BOILED MUTTON (English)

4 tbs. liquor from the meat; 2 tbs. beer; 2 tbs. vinegar; 2 shallots; salt and pepper; butter; flour.

Put into a saucepan the liquor from the boiled mutton, the beer and vinegar, the finely chopped shallots, salt and pepper and a piece of butter the size of a walnut rolled in flour. Stir all together over the heat, bring to the boil, and serve hot.

SAUCE FOR BOILED RABBIT

1 large onion; ½ handful parsley; 1 lettuce; ¼ pint good stock; 1 lemon; butter; flour; salt and pepper; 2 tbs. old ale.

Chop the onion finely, chop the parsley, shred the lettuce and add them to the stock with the juice of the lemon, a piece of butter the size of a walnut rolled in flour, and salt and pepper, and stew all together for half an hour. Then add the dark old ale.

SAUCE FOR BRAISED TONGUE

2 tbs. red-currant jelly; 1 tbs. castor sugar; rind of 2 oranges and 1 lemon; 1 dessertsp. grated horseradish; paprika pepper.

Mix together the red-currant jelly, castor sugar, finely grated orange and lemon rind, grated horseradish and a very little paprika pepper. Stir well and serve.

Use also with cold ham or beef.

SAUCE FOR CALF'S HEAD 1 (English)

1 onion; 2 oz. butter; 1½ oz. flour; 1 pint liquor from boiled calf's head; 1 dessertsp. finely chopped parsley; 1 lemon; salt and pepper.

Brown the sliced onion in the butter, add the flour and brown that too. Moisten with the liquor from the boiled calf's head, and simmer gently for half an hour to reduce it. Strain and add the chopped parsley, the juice and grated rind of the lemon, and salt and pepper to taste.

SAUCE FOR CALF'S HEAD 2 (French)

2 hard-boiled egg yolks; 6 pickled gherkins; capers; 2 shallots; 1 cooked calf's brain; Vinaigrette dressing (p. 28).

Chop very finely together the egg yolks, gherkins, some capers, the shallots and a cooked calf's brain. Now make a Vinaigrette dressing with oil, vinegar, salt, pepper and made mustard, mix in the other ingredients and beat for a little while. It should look like thick cream when finished, and is particularly good when served cold with hot calf's head. The same sauce can be used for hot sheep's head, the sheep's brain then being used.

SAUCE FOR CARP

1 oz. butter; ¼ pint beef gravy; 1 dessertsp. flour; ¼ pint cream; 2 anchovies; lemon juice; Worcestershire sauce.

Mix together over the heat the butter, beef gravy, flour, cream and the finely chopped anchovies. When boiling and thickened, add a squeeze of lemon and a little Worcestershire sauce, just before serving.

SAUCE FOR CARP OR MULLET

½ pint port wine; a little minced parsley and thyme; 1 small onion; 4 anchovies; liver of fish; 2 tbs. vinegar; 1 tbs. ketchup; 3 tbs. gravy; ¼ lb. butter; flour.

Put the port wine into a small stewpan with the parsley, thyme, onion, anchovies, the liver of the fish, the vinegar and ketchup. Let them boil ten minutes and then put in the gravy, the butter and a little flour. Set it on the heat again and keep stirring till it is ready to boil, then strain it through a hair sieve.

SAUCE FOR COLD BEEF

Mix together three tablespoonfuls of oil, two tablespoonfuls of vinegar, one raw egg yolk, chopped parsley, chopped onion, a little chopped tarragon, and salt and pepper. Do not work like a Mayonnaise.

SAUCE FOR COLD GAME (English)

2 hard-boiled egg yolks; 2 tbs. tarragon vinegar; 2 tbs. salad oil; 1 tbs. chilli vinegar; ½ tbs. walnut ketchup; 3 tbs. vinegar; parsley; shallot; pepper and salt; cream.

Rub the hard-boiled egg yolks through a sieve, and add the tarragon vinegar, salad oil, chilli vinegar, walnut ketchup and common vinegar, a small quantity of minced parsley and shallot, and a seasoning of pepper and salt. Add, finally, enough cream to make the sauce the consistency of thick custard.

SAUCE FOR COLD GROUSE

2 egg yolks; 1 tbs. oil; 3 tbs. vinegar; 1 tbs. sugar; 3 tbs. chopped parsley, onion and shallot, mixed; pepper and salt.

Mix the egg yolks very smoothly with the oil, then add the vinegar, sugar, and finely chopped parsley, onion and a little shallot. Add some pepper and salt. Cut up the grouse and pour this sauce over it.

Savoury Sauces

SAUCE FOR EELS (English)

Into a pint of creamy White Sauce (p. 24), stir gradually a table-spoonful of port wine, a teaspoonful of mushroom ketchup and a teaspoonful of the vinegar from pickled onions. Heat through together, stirring, but do not boil.

SAUCE FOR FRIED PIKE

12 button onions; 1 tsp. castor sugar; butter; 2 tbs. sherry; ½ pint Brown Sauce (p. 26); 5 tbs. white stock (p. 33); 12 button mushrooms; ½ tsp. anchovy essence; ½ tsp. ketchup; ½ tsp. Harvey's sauce; cayenne.

Peel the button onions. Put the castor sugar into a saucepan and when it is melted and getting brown, add a piece of butter the size of two walnuts as well as the onions, and shake them over the heat until rather brown. Add the sherry, let it boil, and then add the Brown Sauce and clear stock. Simmer until the onions are quite tender, then add a dozen button mushrooms previously lightly fried, the anchovy essence, ketchup and Harvey's sauce and a touch of cayenne pepper.

SAUCE FOR GOOSE OR DUCK (English)

Two tablespoonfuls of made mustard, the juice of a lemon, a little cayenne and two tablespoonfuls of port wine are all boiled in a saucepan and served hot in a boat.

SAUCE FOR GRILLED PERCH

butter; flour; ½ pint white stock (p. 33); 4 tbs. wine vinegar; 4 tbs. white wine; 1 tbs. chopped shallots; chives; chervil; tarragon.

Make a White Sauce with a large nut of butter, a small spoonful of flour and the stock. While it is simmering gently, put into another pan the wine vinegar, white wine and chopped shallots, and by rapid boiling let the liquid reduce to three tablespoonfuls. Add the White Sauce to this, and simmer on together for five minutes. Finish, off the heat, with two nuts of butter, and a spoonful of chives, chervil and tarragon chopped and mixed together.

SAUCE FOR HAM

Mix together a grated root of horseradish, two ounces of red-currant jelly, a tablespoonful of made mustard, the grated rind and juice of two oranges and of one lemon, and a tablespoonful of white vinegar.

SAUCE FOR HARE

Soak a handful of breadcrumbs in port wine, and heat them with a small lump of butter, a tablespoonful of red-currant jelly, a little salt and a tablespoonful of chilli vinegar. Serve as hot as possible.

SAUCE FOR HOT OR COLD BOILED BEEF

butter; 1 tbs. flour; 4–5 tbs. stock; salt and pepper; cayenne pepper; tarragon; 3 slices lemon; 3 chopped anchovies.

Heat a piece of butter the size of a large walnut, and colour the flour in it. Moisten with the stock, and add salt and pepper, a little cayenne pepper, chopped tarragon, the slices of lemon and the anchovies. Cook all together for a few minutes, then take out the lemon, strain the sauce, and serve it with boiled fresh beef.

SAUCE FOR ROAST BEEF (English)

Beat the yolk of a hard-boiled egg with a little dry mustard, salt, pepper and vinegar, add a tablespoonful of grated horseradish, and stir well together to serve.

SAUCE FOR ROAST HARE

brown roux (p. 25); 1 onion; 1 shallot; a bouquet of parsley, thyme and 1 bayleaf; 1 dessertsp. vinegar; ½ pint stock; liver and blood of hare; lemon juice or vinegar.

Make a little brown roux, and add to it the chopped onion and shallot, the bouquet of herbs, the vinegar and the stock. Bring to the boil, and stirring let it reduce and thicken. Just before serving take out the bouquet and add the finely chopped liver of the hare, and its blood, which has been mixed with a little lemon juice or vinegar to prevent it from coagulating. Stir and cook for two or three minutes and serve. The sauce should be well seasoned.

SAUCE FOR ROAST RABBIT (French)

butter; 2–3 onions; salt and pepper; blood of rabbit; lemon juice or vinegar.

Put a piece of butter the size of an egg into a saucepan, and add the onions cut up finely, salt and pepper and six tablespoonfuls of water. Boil for half an hour. Then add the blood of the rabbit (which you have mixed with a little lemon juice or vinegar to prevent it from coagulating), heat the sauce up again without boiling and serve it hot, first straining it if you wish.

SAUCE FOR ROAST MEAT 1

Boil up a half-and-half mixture of stock and red wine (about half a pint in all) with a few chopped shallots and crushed anchovies added. Simmer, pass through a sieve and add the gravy from the joint, with lastly a few drops of lemon.

SAUCE FOR ROAST MEAT 2

1 onion; 2–3 cloves garlic; 1 sprig thyme; 1 bayleaf; ½ lemon; ¼ pint ale; ¼ pint vinegar; ½ pint good stock; salt and pepper; flour.

Put the thinly sliced onion, garlic, thyme, bayleaf and thinly sliced lemon into a saucepan with the ale, vinegar and stock; season to taste with salt and pepper, bring to the boil and simmer for half an hour. Then thicken with flour and serve with any roast meat.

SAUCE FOR ROAST MEAT 3

Stew together a glass of old ale, and the same of stock, one anchovy, a sliced shallot, the juice of a Seville orange and a little nutmeg. Strain and mix with some of the gravy from the meat.

SAUCE FOR ROAST MUTTON (English)

Boil up the gravy from the mutton, seasoned with nutmeg, the juice of an orange and a little claret.

SAUCE FOR ROAST VEAL (English)

flour; 1 wineglass claret; nutmeg; elder vinegar; orange.

After roasting the veal thicken the gravy in the pan with a little flour, brown it a little, and moisten with hot water. Then add the claret, some grated nutmeg, a little elder vinegar and two or three slices of orange. Boil up, stirring well, and strain.

SAUCE FOR SEAKALE (English)

1 oz. butter; 1 tbs. flour; ¼ pint milk; salt; 2 tbs. cream; celery essence.

Melt the butter in a stewpan, add the flour, and stir over the heat till smooth. Next add the milk and boil for ten minutes, skimming all the time. Add a little salt, the cream and two drops only of celery essence, and pour the sauce over the seakale.

SAUCE FOR SOLE 1

2 hard-boiled egg yolks; 1 raw egg yolk; cream; 1 tbs. tarragon vinegar; salt and pepper.

Mix together the hard-boiled egg yolks, raw yolk, a little cream and the tarragon vinegar. When quite smooth put the mixture into a saucepan, heat up without boiling, and season it with salt and pepper before pouring over the fillets of sole.

SAUCE FOR SOLE 2

1 handful mixed basil, parsley and thyme; 1 shallot; 1 soup-ladle clear gravy or consommé; 1 tbs. white wine or white wine vinegar; juice of 1 lemon; salt and pepper.

Mince very finely the basil, parsley, thyme and shallot, add the gravy or consommé, white wine or white wine vinegar, lemon juice, and salt and pepper to taste. Mix well together and serve very hot.

SAUCE FOR STEAK

⅛ pint red wine; ⅛ pint ketchup; butter; pepper; 1 tsp. shallot vinegar.

Take equal parts of red wine and ketchup, a small piece of butter, a little pepper and the shallot vinegar, and heat through in a small saucepan. Pour over the steak on serving.

Use also with mutton chops.

SAUCE FOR STURGEON (English)

1 anchovy; 2 oz. butter; 2 oz. flour; anchovy-flavoured water; meat of 1 small cooked crab or lobster; a few picked shrimps; 2 tbs. mushroom ketchup; 2 tbs. white wine; lemon juice.

Cook the chopped anchovy in a very little water until it is quite soft, then strain off the liquid and add enough water to make three quarters of a pint. Now make a roux with the butter and flour, and moisten it with the anchovy-flavoured water, adding the crab or lobster meat chopped up very fine, the shrimps, mushroom ketchup and white wine. Boil all together for a few minutes, then add a squeeze of lemon at the last.

SAUCE FOR VENISON I (English)

Boil an ounce of currants in a little water for a few minutes, then add three tablespoonfuls of breadcrumbs, a piece of butter the size of a walnut, four cloves and a glass of port wine. Stir together until boiling, and serve hot.

SAUCE FOR VENISON 2

Boil together a quarter of a pint of old ale, the same of water and the same of vinegar, an onion stuck with cloves, two anchovies, salt and pepper. When ready, strain and serve.

SAUCE FOR WILD DUCK (English)

Boil together for a few minutes a tablespoonful each of walnut ketchup, Worcestershire sauce, lemon juice and port wine, a blade of mace, a touch of cayenne pepper and eight tablespoonfuls of gravy. Pour over the bird on serving.

SAUCE FOR WOOD PIGEON (English)

3–4 livers of the birds; ½ pint stock or gravy; 2 egg yolks; thyme; parsley; nutmeg; cayenne.

For this take the livers of three or four of the birds, boil and pass them through a wire sieve. Add the stock or good gravy, the egg yolks and a little chopped thyme and parsley; season with a little grated nutmeg and cayenne. Serve hot in a sauce-boat.

SAVOURY SAUCE

butter; 1½ tbs. flour; ½ pint water in which asparagus has been cooked; 2 tbs. mixed parsley, tarragon, chives and cress.

Make a White Sauce (p. 24) with a tablespoonful of butter, the flour
and the water in which the asparagus has been cooked. Cook, stirring
now and then, for twenty minutes, and then add two tablespoonfuls
of a mixture of chopped parsley, tarragon, chives and cress which
have first been stewed in a little butter.

Use with asparagus.

SAVOURY MAYONNAISE SAUCE (American)

Add an eighth of a teaspoonful each of dry mustard, paprika pepper
and Worcestershire sauce, first mixed well together, to four fl. ounces
of Mayonnaise Sauce (p. 28).

Use with fish, meat or vegetable salads.

SAVOURY MUSTARD SAUCE (American)

To half a pint of Brown Sauce (p. 26) add three dessertspoonfuls of
grated horseradish and the same of made mustard.

Use with boiled beef or lamb.

SAVOURY CIDER SAUCE (American)

*1 slice onion; 1 tbs. sweet green pepper; 3 dessertsp. pork fat; 3 dessertsp.
flour; ½ pint cider; 1–2 tsp. mustard pickle.*

Slightly brown the minced slice of onion, the chopped sweet green
pepper and the pork fat, then stir in the flour and brown that too.
Then gradually add the cider and cook for five minutes or until the
sauce is thick and creamy. Finish with the mustard pickle.

Use with ham.

SAVOURY CREAM SAUCE

To half a pint of Cream Sauce (p. 62) add a teaspoonful each of
chopped onion, parsley, sweet red pepper and celery.

Use with pork or lamb.

SAVOURY CUSTARD SAUCE

2 oz. fresh butter; 2 tbs. flour; ½ pint chicken broth; 1 onion; parsley; peppercorns; cloves; ½ pint milk; salt; cayenne; 2–3 egg yolks; lemon juice.

Put the butter to melt in a saucepan and stir in the flour to make a roux. Next add the chicken broth which you have flavoured with onions, parsley, peppercorns and a few cloves, and also the milk. Stir all well together to prevent it from getting lumpy, till it boils. Flavour with a little salt and cayenne. Strain and mix in the egg yolks and add a squeeze of lemon juice.

Use with boiled chicken.

SHALLOT SAUCE

Fry six small shallots in a tablespoonful of butter, with a dessert-spoonful of flour, and when they are browned, add half a pint of fish stock (p. 34) with a bouquet of parsley, thyme and bayleaf. Simmer for half an hour or so, then strain.

Use with bream.

SHRIMP SAUCE 1 (Sauce Crevettes)

This sauce can be made with either White Wine Sauce (p. 179) or Hollandaise Sauce (p. 27). In either case, finish with two ounces of Shrimp Butter (p. 188) and an ounce of small shelled shrimps for each three quarters of a pint of the sauce. The colour of the sauce should be a fresh pale pink.

Use with fish.

SHRIMP SAUCE 2

½ pint cooked shrimps; butter; flour; cayenne; anchovy essence; picked shrimps.

Pound the cooked shrimps, shells and all, and boil them for ten minutes in half a pint of water. Pass through a hair sieve into a sauce-pan and add a piece of butter the size of two walnuts which you have kneaded with a good teaspoonful of flour. Stir until the sauce thickens, and season with a little cayenne pepper and a teaspoonful of anchovy essence. Garnish with a few picked shrimps.

Use as above.

SHRIMP SAUCE 3

shrimps; ½ pint milk; bayleaf; mace; lemon juice; anchovy essence; cayenne.

Shell enough shrimps to make a quarter of a pint of the tails and make a fish stock with the shells by cooking them in the milk with a bayleaf and a blade of mace. Use this stock to make half a pint of White Sauce (p. 24), and when it is ready add the shrimps, whole or chopped; cook for a few minutes and then finish with a squeeze of lemon juice and a teaspoonful of anchovy essence. A dash of cayenne pepper also helps.

Use as above.

SORREL SAUCE 1

Add a good tablespoonful of sorrel purée to a White Sauce (p. 24), stir and mix well, and finish with a little butter.
Use with roast chicken or veal.

SORREL SAUCE 2 (Hungarian)

1 lb. sorrel leaves; 1 oz. fat; 1 oz. flour; 1 egg.

Wash the sorrel leaves, chop them up finely, put them into the hot fat, and then add the flour and stir and cook until the flour is golden-brown. Add water to make the right consistency, stir until quite smooth, and cook gently for an hour. Just before serving add a beaten egg.

Use as above.

SORREL SAUCE 3

Pick over a small handful of sorrel, cover it with cold water, bring to the boil, and cook for a few minutes. Drain well, chop up finely, and add it to half a pint of gravy which you have already heated up.

Use as above.

Savoury Sauces

SOUR SAUCE 1 (American)

scant ½ pint highly seasoned fish stock (p. 34); juice of 1 large lemon; salt and pepper; 2 egg yolks; 1 tbs. flour; 1 tbs. chopped almonds; 2 tsp. capers.

Put the stock into a saucepan with the lemon juice, and salt and pepper. Mix the egg yolks with the flour, pour the boiling stock over them in a double saucepan and let this thicken, stirring all the time. Then add the chopped almonds and capers.

Use with boiled or baked fish.

SOUR SAUCE 2 (American)

To half a pint of Brown Sauce (p. 26) add three dessertspoonfuls of chopped pickled cucumber.

Use with cold beef and pork.

SOUR CREAM SAUCE (American)

½ pint double sour cream; 3 dessertsp. vinegar; 3 level tsp. sugar; 1 level tsp. salt; 1 level tsp. dry mustard; ¼ tsp. paprika pepper.

Whip up the cream until it reaches the consistency of custard, then beating lightly, gradually add a mixture of the vinegar, sugar, salt, dry mustard and paprika pepper.

Use with cold beef, pork or tongue.

SPANISH SAUCE (American)

onion; green sweet pepper; 2 tbs. fat; 1 lb. tin tomatoes; salt and pepper; 1 tsp. oregano.

Chop up a tablespoonful each of onion and green sweet pepper and cook them slowly in the fat for about five minutes. Then add the tomatoes, salt and pepper, oregano, and simmer until the sauce is thick. Strain and serve.

Use with beef, mutton or veal.

SUGO

marrow from 1 beefbone; butter; 3 chicken livers; 3 oz. minced veal; ½ lb. mixed and chopped parsley, celery, carrots, onion, tomato, soaked dried mushrooms; salt and pepper; flour; ½ glass each dry white wine and stock.

Cook together in a little butter the marrow, chicken livers and veal, all finely chopped; add the vegetables, salt and pepper, and a dredging of flour, then add the wine and stock. Let the sauce simmer until it has thickened and the pieces of meat and liver are almost melted, then pass it through a fine hair sieve or muslin.

Use with macaroni and other pastas or rice..

SULTANA SAUCE

2 oz. sultanas; sherry; sugar; glaze.

Swell the sultanas in enough sherry to cover; next put them in a stew-pan on the heat; add sugar to sweeten and a piece of glaze the size of half an egg. Just melt and mix well; it should on no account be allowed to boil. Add these ingredients to the gravy of your pork.

Use with roast pork or sucking pig.

TARRAGON SAUCE I

Reduce a pint of stock to half-glaze, and add to it a bunch of tarragon leaves and a tablespoonful of water. Boil up, then strain, and add a little tarragon vinegar and a few fresh tarragon leaves chopped small.

Use with fish.

TARRAGON SAUCE 2

Chop up a handful of tarragon leaves and boil them for five minutes in a little water. Mix them with half a pint of Béchamel Sauce (p. 24), and season with salt and cayenne pepper.

Use with boiled fowl.

TARRAGON SAUCE 3

Whip lightly half a pint of double cream seasoned with salt and pepper and lastly mix in a little finely chopped fresh tarragon and chervil.

Use with hot roast chicken.

TARTARE SAUCE (Hot)

4 tbs. White Sauce (p. 24); 4 tbs. milk or stock; 2 tbs. Sauce Tartare (p. 152).

Put the White Sauce into a saucepan, add the milk or stock, and boil together for a few minutes. Then add the Sauce Tartare, stir very quickly with a wooden spoon making the sauce as hot as possible without boiling it and serve.

Use with calf's head.

TEXAS SAUCE

Flavour three quarters of a pint of Curry Sauce (p. 66) just before serving with a teaspoonful of lemon juice, half a teaspoonful of chopped parsley, a good pinch of saffron and last of all an ounce of butter whisked in by small pieces.

Use with curried fish or meat.

THOUSAND ISLAND DRESSING (American)

To four tablespoonfuls of Mayonnaise Sauce (p. 28) add three dessertspoonfuls of Chilli Sauce (p. 58), a good teaspoonful each of ketchup, vinegar, chives, chopped green and red peppers and half a teaspoonful of paprika pepper.

Use with vegetable salads.

TOMATO AND MUSHROOM SAUCE

To half a pint of any plain Tomato Sauce (p. 170), add two ounces of sliced fried or tinned mushrooms.

Use for heating up meat.

TOMATO SAUCE 1 (Simple)

3½ lb. fresh ripe tomatoes; 1½ oz. butter or 3 tbs. olive oil; pinch of salt and freshly ground black pepper; 1 sprig parsley; ½ clove garlic.

Cut the tomatoes in halves, unskinned, and press out the seeds. Heat the butter or oil in a pan and add the tomatoes, parsley, garlic and seasoning. Put on the lid, simmer for thirty to thirty-five minutes only, then strain finely with a little pressure on the tomatoes and garlic, if you like to accentuate the taste of the latter. Cover with a little melted butter if you do not want to use the sauce at once.

Escoffier, whose recipe this is, says that this has the advantage of being quick and preserving all the freshness and flavour of the fruit. He adds that if you cannot get fresh tomatoes, they can be replaced by tinned ones, which are dealt with in the same way.

TOMATO SAUCE 2 (Hungarian)

2 lb. ripe tomatoes; ½ oz. each chopped onion and parsley; 2 oz. lard; 1 oz. butter; 1 oz. flour; stock; salt and pepper; lemon juice; sugar; 1 tbs. red wine.

Stew the sliced tomatoes with the chopped onion and parsley in lard with a very little water. Cook until this is a thick pulp, then pass it through a sieve. Thicken this with a roux made with the butter and flour, and add a little stock. Season with salt and pepper, and cook for twenty minutes or so. Then flavour with lemon juice, a touch of sugar and the red wine.

Use for any tomato-flavoured sauce as required.

TOMATO SAUCE 3 (Italian)

¼ onion; ½ stick celery; few leaves of basil; bunch of parsley; 4 tbs. pure olive oil; salt and pepper; 8–9 ripe tomatoes.

Mince finely the onion, celery, basil and parsley. Add the olive oil, a pinch of salt and pepper and the tomatoes cut in slices. Boil all together until the sauce is thick and creamy and then strain through a sieve and serve.

Use as above.

TOMATO SAUCE 4 (Italian)

2 lbs. ripe tomatoes; a little chopped onion, carrot, celery, basil, thyme and parsley; salt.

Chop up the tomatoes, and put them into a saucepan with the chopped vegetables and herbs. Bring to the boil and simmer gently for about two hours. Rub this purée through a sieve and on reheating season with salt.

Use as above.

TOMATO SAUCE 5 (Italian)

oil or butter; ham; onion; celery; parsley; thyme; bayleaf; 1 tbs. flour; 2½ lb. ripe tomatoes; salt; sugar.

Melt a little oil or butter in a saucepan and add a little chopped ham, half fat and half lean. Brown this lightly, then add a little chopped onion and celery with a few sprigs of parsley and thyme and a bayleaf; brown these too, then stir in the flour. When this has browned, add the chopped tomatoes, bring to the boil when they have exuded their juice, and simmer together for two hours. Rub the purée through a sieve, and heat up with a seasoning of salt and a little sugar.

Use as above.

TOMATO SAUCE 6

1 oz. butter; 2 oz. lean ham; 2 shallots; salt and pepper; 1 bayleaf; sprig of thyme; leaf of rosemary; 10 peppercorns; 1 lb. tomatoes; 1 tbs. flour.

Melt the butter in a saucepan, and cook in it without browning the ham cut small and the chopped shallots. Add salt and pepper, a bayleaf, a sprig of thyme, a leaf of rosemary if available, the peppercorns and sliced tomatoes. Sprinkle over the flour and cook all together for about twenty minutes or until the sauce is well reduced. Then sieve finely, correct the seasoning and serve.

Use as above.

TOMATO SAUCE 7

1½ lb. tomatoes; ¼ pint stock; 1 small sliced onion; parsley; thyme; bayleaf; salt and pepper; 1 oz. butter; ½ oz. flour; sugar.

Cut the tomatoes in halves, squeeze out the juice and strain it into a small basin. Put the tomato-halves into a saucepan, with the stock, onion, a bouquet of parsley, thyme and bayleaf and a little salt and pepper, simmer gently for an hour, then pass through a fine sieve. Make a roux with the butter and flour, moisten with the sieved tomatoes, and thin down to the right consistency with some of the tomato juice. Season to taste, adding a little sugar, and reheat.

Use as above.

TOMATO CHEESE SAUCE

To half a pint of Tomato Sauce (p. 170) add six tablespoonfuls of grated cheese and a teaspoonful of made mustard. Serve when the cheese is melted.

Use with fish or eggs.

TOMATO CREAM SAUCE (American)

1 lb. tomatoes; 1 sprig thyme; 1 stick celery; 1 slice onion; 1 small piece bayleaf; salt; cayenne; ¼ level tsp. bicarbonate of soda; ½ pint White Sauce (p. 24).

Chop the tomatoes and stew for twenty minutes with the thyme, celery, onion, bayleaf, and salt and cayenne pepper to taste. Rub through a conical sieve and add to the White Sauce with the bicarbonate of soda. The soda is included to prevent the tomato from curdling the milk.

Use with fish, eggs and poultry.

TOMATO SHERRY SAUCE (American)

To half a pint of Tomato Sauce (p. 170) add four tablespoonfuls of sherry.

Use with fish.

TOULOUSE SAUCE

Add to a pint of Hollandaise Sauce (p. 27) two tablespoonfuls of dry white wine, a sliced truffle and six minced mushrooms which have been lightly fried and well drained. Just before serving add a little meat glaze (p. 33).

Use with beefsteak.

TUNNY FISH SAUCE (Italian)

2 oz. tunny fish; 2 anchovies in oil; 2 oz. capers; 3–4 sprigs parsley; 1 hard-boiled egg yolk; olive oil; juice of ½ lemon; pepper.

Chop up the tunny fish, anchovies, capers and parsley, and pound them to a smooth paste in a mortar with the egg yolk and just enough olive oil to moisten them. Now add up to half a pint of olive oil very slowly in the same manner as you would make a Mayonnaise (p. 28). Add the juice of half a lemon and a little pepper. The sauce should be fairly liquid.

Use with boiled veal (cold), vitello tonnato.

VEAL GRAVY TOMATÉE

Add to half a pint of veal stock (p. 32) an ounce of tomato purée and an eighth of a pint of tomato juice. Reduce by a fifth and strain through a cloth.

Use with roast veal.

VEGETABLE SAUCE (Czechoslovakian)

½ lb. mixed carrot, turnip, celery and parsnip; ½ oz. butter; 3 tbs. flour; 1 pint stock or thin gravy; salt and pepper; mace or nutmeg.

Cut up the vegetables into small dice. Put these into a saucepan with butter, cover, and let them sweat on a low heat for about five minutes without browning. Now add the flour and cook on for a minute or two, mixing well. Moisten with the stock or thin gravy and season with salt, pepper and a little ground mace or nutmeg. Cook on for a quarter of an hour, and the sauce is ready.

Use with roast meat or chicken.

VENISON SAUCE

This is a Poivrade Sauce (p. 110) finished, for each pint of the sauce, with two tablespoonfuls of red-currant jelly previously melted and mixed with five tablespoonfuls of cream. This addition must be made off the heat.

VINAIGRETTE SAUCE I

Basic sauce (see p. 28).

VINAIGRETTE SAUCE 2

2 hard-boiled egg yolks; gherkins; capers; 2 raw shallots; oil; vinegar; salt and pepper; made mustard.

Chop together the egg yolks, a few gherkins and capers and the shallots. Make an ordinary vinaigrette dressing (p. 28) of oil, vinegar, salt and pepper, adding a little made mustard, and mix all well together.

Use with hot game, calf's head, salad, asparagus or cauliflower.

VINAIGRETTE SAUCE 3 (American)

To eight tablespoonfuls of ordinary French Dressing (p. 28) add, in this order, a tablespoonful of chopped green peppers, a teaspoonful each of chopped chives, parsley and capers, and a tablespoonful of chopped pickled cucumber. Stir well together.

Use with beef, lamb, or calf's head.

VINAIGRETTE SAUCE 4 (American)

1 level tsp. salt; ¼ level tsp. paprika pepper; pepper; 3 tsp. tarragon vinegar; 3 dessertsp. cider vinegar; 4½ tbs. olive oil; 3 tsp. each chopped sweet green pepper and pickled cucumber; 1 tsp. each parsley and chives.

Mix together the salt, paprika, and a dash of ordinary pepper, tarragon vinegar, cider vinegar and olive oil, adding the chopped sweet green pepper, pickled cucumber and finely chopped parsley and chives.

Use as above.

Vinaigrette Sauce Variations

The Americans are far more addicted to salad-eating than we are, and this has given them the chance to prove their inventiveness in the field of providing sauces (dressings) to eat with them. Mayonnaises will be found on pp. 92–6; here follow the Vinaigrettes.

The quantities of the ingredients apply to eight tablespoons of the sauce. Spoonfuls are level.

Anchovy Vinaigrette Sauce. Add two teaspoonfuls of anchovy paste creamed with a little of the sauce and three teaspoonfuls each of chopped parsley and minced onion, preferably spring onions.

Breslin French Vinaigrette Sauce. Add three teaspoonfuls of chopped blanched pistachio nuts and half a teaspoonful of finely chopped truffle.

California Vinaigrette Sauce. In making the sauce use either lemon or grapefruit juice instead of the usual vinegar.

Cheese and Egg Vinaigrette Sauce. Add three teaspoonfuls each of chopped parsley and sweet red pepper, three tablespoonfuls of chopped white cheese, e.g. Cheddar, and one chopped hard-boiled egg.

Chiffonade Vinaigrette Sauce. Add three teaspoonfuls each of chopped green and red sweet peppers, chopped green olives and pickled cucumber and one chopped hard-boiled egg.

Chutney Vinaigrette Sauce. Add three dessertspoonfuls of drained chopped chutney.

Cream Vinaigrette Sauce. Add three dessertspoonfuls of cream or sour cream.

Cumberland Vinaigrette Sauce. Make the dressing with lemon juice instead of vinegar and add three teaspoonfuls each of red-currant jelly and double cream and a quarter of a teaspoonful of grated lemon rind.

Curry Vinaigrette Sauce. Add a quarter of a teaspoonful of curry powder, a little salt and, if you like, a few drops of onion juice.

Fruit Vinaigrette Sauce. Make the sauce with lemon juice instead of vinegar and add a pinch of nutmeg and chopped or powdered dried marjoram and a quarter of a teaspoonful of chervil.

Fruit Juice Vinaigrette Sauce. Use a mixture of three parts grapefruit, orange or pineapple juice and one part lemon instead of vinegar when making the sauce.

Ginger Vinaigrette Sauce. Add three teaspoonfuls of finely minced preserved ginger.

Honey Vinaigrette Sauce. Add two tablespoonfuls of honey to the sauce, leaving out the pepper, and beat until frothy.

Horseradish Vinaigrette Sauce. Add three teaspoonfuls of scraped or grated horseradish.

Italian Vinaigrette Sauce. Add three teaspoonfuls of tomato purée or ketchup and a small minced green sweet pepper.

Lime Vinaigrette Sauce. Use equal parts of lime and lemon juice instead of the usual vinegar.

Martinique Vinaigrette Sauce. Add a teaspoonful of finely chopped parsley and three teaspoonfuls of finely chopped green sweet pepper.

Mint Vinaigrette Sauce. Add three teaspoonfuls of chopped fresh mint.

Miramar Vinaigrette Sauce. Add three chopped anchovy fillets, a chopped hard-boiled egg and half a teaspoonful of chopped chives.

Mustard Vinaigrette Sauce. Make the sauce with a teaspoonful of dry mustard and a pinch of cayenne pepper in addition to the seasoning.

Piquant Vinaigrette Sauce. Add three teaspoonfuls of chopped green olives and half a teaspoonful each of chopped capers and red sweet peppers.

Porto Rico Vinaigrette Sauce. Use half lemon juice and half wine vinegar in making the sauce and add three dessertspoonfuls of chopped green olives and three teaspoonfuls of tomato ketchup.

Roquefort Vinaigrette Sauce. 1. Add one to three tablespoonfuls of crumbled dry Roquefort cheese and a few drops of onion juice.
  2. Cream half a teacupful of soft Roquefort cheese with a little of the sauce and stir in the rest by degrees.

Russian Vinaigrette Sauce. Add three dessertspoonfuls of mild chilli sauce, three teaspoonfuls of finely chopped red or green sweet peppers and a dash of onion juice.

Spanish Vinaigrette Sauce. Add half a teaspoonful of mild chilli powder and the same of dry mustard to the dry ingredients.

Spiced Vinaigrette Sauce. Add three teaspoonfuls of finely scraped or grated horseradish, a quarter of a teaspoonful of mustard, half a teaspoonful of chopped chives, three teaspoonfuls of chopped parsley and one finely minced shallot.

Swiss Vinaigrette Sauce. Add a quarter of a teaspoonful of mustard, three tablespoonfuls of grated Gruyère cheese and a quarter of a teaspoonful of Worcestershire sauce.

Thousand Island Vinaigrette Sauce. Make the sauce with an egg yolk, eight tablespoonfuls of oil, the juice of half an orange and half a lemon, a teaspoonful of salt, a quarter of a teaspoonful of paprika pepper, a teaspoonful of onion juice, three teaspoonfuls of chopped parsley, eight sliced stuffed olives, a teaspoonful of Worcestershire sauce and a quarter of a teaspoonful of mustard.

Tomato Vinaigrette Sauce. Add a teaspoonful of strained tomato juice and a little onion juice.

VINEGAR SAUCE (American)

8 tbs. vinegar; 3 level tsp. brown sugar; 2 cloves; mace; bayleaf; cinnamon; allspice; salt; paprika pepper.

Simmer the vinegar with the brown sugar, cloves, a blade of mace, half a bayleaf, a half-inch stick of cinnamon, two whole allspice, a quarter of a level teaspoonful of salt and a dash of paprika pepper. After ten minutes, strain the liquid.

Use hot or cold with pigs' trotters.

WALNUT GRAVY

1 tsp. butter; 2 tbs. grated walnuts; 1 pint stock or thin gravy; onion; 1 tbs. flour; salt and pepper.

Melt the butter and fry the grated walnuts in it until they are a dark brown. Then add the stock or thin gravy, and half an onion, and simmer all together for twenty minutes. Take out the onion, and stir in the flour mixed smoothly with a little cold gravy, season to taste with salt and pepper, cook for another ten minutes, then strain again and serve.

Use with lamb.

WALNUT SAUCE 1 (Flemish)

Make a thick sauce with half a pint of gravy, then break up two or three pickled walnuts in one or two tablespoonfuls of their pickle, and add them to the sauce.

Use with lamb.

WALNUT SAUCE 2 (Russian)

about 20 fresh walnuts; 1 tsp. French mustard; 2 hard-boiled egg yolks; 1 tbs. fine brown breadcrumbs; 1 tbs. oil; ¼ pint vinegar.

Shell, skin and pound the walnuts in a mortar, adding the French mustard, egg yolks, fine brown breadcrumbs, oil and vinegar. Mix all well together.

Use with boiled or fried fish.

WATERCRESS SAUCE

1 handful watercress; 2 egg yolks; juice of 1 lemon; castor sugar.

Simmer the watercress in a little water and press out the juice through a sieve. Take a teacupful of this juice, season it, and add the egg yolks which have been well beaten with the lemon juice mixed with a little castor sugar. Stir in a double boiler until the sauce thickens.

Use with boiled chicken.

WHITE WINE SAUCE (Sauce Vin Blanc)

¾ pint fish Velouté (p. 24); 4 tbs. fish fumet (p. 34); 2 egg yolks; butter; cream.

Add the fish fumet to the fish Velouté and bind with the egg yolks. Finish with butter and a little fresh cream. The reduced poaching liquor of the fish which it is to accompany should always be incorporated in this sauce.

Use with fish.

WINE SAUCE 1

Four tablespoonfuls of white wine and three of vinegar, a large onion and four anchovies are simmered for an hour and strained. Add eight tablespoonfuls of cream, thickened with a little flour and butter, and stir over gentle heat.

Use with salmon or freshwater fish.

WINE SAUCE 2

butter; flour; ½ pint good stock; thyme; mace; 1 anchovy; 4 cloves; 2 shallots; 1 dessertsp. lobster spawn; 1 wineglass sherry or Madeira; fish liquor.

Melt some butter in a saucepan, add some flour to make a good roux; cook and mix it with great care. Put the stock, a little thyme, a blade of mace, the anchovy, cloves, shallots and lobster spawn in a pan, bring to the boil and simmer for half an hour. Make a roux with some butter and flour. Strain the stock and add to the roux. Stir, and when it is well blended, add the sherry or Madeira and the liquor that came from the fish.

If for grey mullet, you must leave out the spawn.

Use with red or grey mullet.

WINE SAUCE 3

1 glass port; 1 tbs. each mushroom ketchup, Harvey's sauce, lemon juice and finely minced onion; 2 tsp. brown sugar; salt; pepper; mace or nutmeg.

Put into a saucepan the port, mushroom ketchup, Harvey's sauce, lemon juice, finely minced onion, brown sugar, salt and pepper and mace or nutmeg to taste. Heat through over hot water for ten minutes, stirring all the time, then strain and serve.

Use with wild fowl.

WYVERN SAUCE

$\frac{1}{2}$ *oz. butter;* $\frac{1}{2}$ *oz. flour;* $\frac{1}{4}$ *pint beef gravy;* $\frac{1}{2}$ *glass sherry; 1 tsp. caramel; 1 tbs. mushroom ketchup; 1 tbs. Harvey's sauce;* $1\frac{1}{2}$ *tbs. Anchovy Sauce (p. 41).*

Melt the butter in a small saucepan, mix in the flour; stir in, when the butter and flour have amalgamated, the beef gravy, sherry, caramel, mushroom ketchup, Harvey's sauce and Anchovy Sauce. Stir and heat well before serving.

Use with beef or game.

YORKSHIRE SAUCE

1 orange; $\frac{1}{4}$ *pint port wine; 1 tbs. Half-Glaze Sauce (p. 26); 1 tbs. red-currant jelly; cinnamon; cayenne pepper.*

Blanch a dessertspoonful of thinly shredded orange rind in the port for a few minutes, then strain it from the shreds, putting them aside. Add to the wine the Half-Glaze Sauce, red-currant jelly and a pinch each of cinnamon and cayenne pepper, boil for a second or two and then strain. Finally add the orange shreds and the strained juice of the orange.

Serve with braised ham or duck.

Savoury Butters

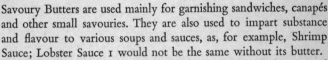

Savoury Butters are used mainly for garnishing sandwiches, canapés and other small savouries. They are also used to impart substance and flavour to various soups and sauces, as, for example, Shrimp Sauce; Lobster Sauce 1 would not be the same without its butter.

Maître d'Hôtel Butter in a pat is used to garnish grilled meat, and Anchovy Butter is used with fried and grilled fish.

ALMOND BUTTER 1 (Beurre d'Amandes)

Four ounces of blanched and skinned Jordan almonds are pounded to a fine paste with a few drops of water. Mix with six ounces of butter and pass through a fine sieve.

ALMOND BUTTER 2 (American)

Fry four ounces of blanched and shredded almonds in the same amount of butter until the almonds are delicately browned, stirring all the time.

Use with fish.

ANCHOVY BUTTER (Beurre d'Anchois)

Two ounces of fillets of salted anchovies are washed and pounded with four ounces of butter. Pass through a fine sieve.

ANCHOVY-ROQUEFORT BUTTER (American)

To four tablespoonfuls of creamed butter, add a teaspoonful each of vinegar, anchovy paste and made mustard and two teaspoonfuls of Roquefort cheese. Blend smoothly together.

Use with grilled fish.

BERCY BUTTER

Put into a small saucepan an eighth of a pint of white wine and half an ounce of finely chopped blanched shallots. Reduce the wine by half, then add a quarter of a pound of creamed butter, half a teaspoonful of chopped parsley, an ounce of poached beef marrow cut in cubes, and salt, pepper and a drop of lemon juice. This butter must not be quite melted.

Use with grilled beef.

BLACK BUTTER 1 (Beurre Noir)

Cook the butter in a frying-pan until it just begins to turn brown, no more, or it will burn and taste bitter. Finish with a few drops of vinegar swilled in the pan.

BLACK BUTTER 2

Cook the butter until it begins to turn brown, then add a little vinegar and chopped parsley. Some add a few capers as well.

BLOATER BUTTER (Beurre de Hareng Saur)

See Herring Butter (p. 184), but use bloaters instead of herrings.

CAVIARE BUTTER (Beurre de Caviar)

Pound two ounces of caviare very well indeed. When it is quite smooth add six ounces of butter and pass through a fine sieve.

CHEESE BUTTER

Mix together four tablespoonfuls of creamed butter with an equal amount of soft, strongly flavoured white cheese.

CHILLI BUTTER

Incorporate three dessertspoonfuls of Chilli Sauce (p. 58) with four tablespoonfuls creamed butter.

CHIVES BUTTER

To four tablespoonfuls of creamed butter add three teaspoonfuls of finely minced chives and a teaspoonful of lemon juice.

Savoury Butters

CHIVRY BUTTER (Beurre Chivry)

A handful of chopped parsley, shallot, tarragon, chives and burnet
are blanched, plunged into cold water and then pressed dry. Pound,
mix with six tablespoonfuls of butter and pass through a sieve.

CHUTNEY BUTTER

Mix three teaspoonfuls of chutney with four tablespoonfuls of
creamed butter.

COLBERT BUTTER (Beurre Colbert)

Add to Maître d'Hôtel Butter (p. 185) a dessertspoonful of melted
meat glaze (p. 33) for every four ounces of the butter. If a *maigre*
butter is wanted, the meat glaze can be replaced by fish glaze (p. 35),
or fish fumet (p. 34), reduced until it is a syrup.

CRAYFISH BUTTER (Beurre d'Écrevisses)

The heads and shells of crayfish are cooked with an ordinary mirepoix
(p. 36) and, when cold, pounded finely with an equal weight of
butter, and passed through a fine sieve.

EGG BUTTER

To three ounces of creamed butter add two mashed hard-boiled
egg yolks, half a teaspoonful of lemon juice, a dash of Tabasco sauce
and a seasoning of salt and cayenne pepper.

FILBERT BUTTER (Beurre d'Avelines)

See Almond Butter (p. 181), but use filberts instead of almonds.

GARLIC BUTTER (Beurre d'Ail)

Blanched garlic well pounded and mixed with an equal quantity of
butter. Pass through a fine sieve.

GREEN BUTTER (Beurre Vert)

See Montpellier Butter (p. 185).

GREEN SAVOURY BUTTER (American)

Mix together three tablespoonfuls of cold spinach purée, a table-spoonful of anchovy paste, a teaspoonful of chopped capers, a dash of paprika and salt to taste. Rub through a sieve, mix well and add to six tablespoonfuls of creamed butter.

HAZEL-NUT BUTTER (Beurre de Noisettes)

See Almond Butter (p. 181), but use slightly dried hazel-nuts instead of almonds.

HERRING BUTTER (Beurre de Hareng)

Skinned raw fillets of herring pounded with twice as much butter as herring. Pass through a sieve.

HORSERADISH BUTTER (Beurre de Raifort)

Add a dessertspoonful of very finely grated horseradish to five ounces of softened butter.

KETCHUP BUTTER

To four tablespoonfuls of creamed butter add three dessertspoonfuls of ketchup.

LEMON BUTTER

Clarify four tablespoonfuls of fresh butter, season it and flavour it with lemon juice.

LOBSTER BUTTER 1 (Beurre de Homard)

Pound the eggs, coral and creamy parts of a lobster with an equal quantity of butter, and pass through a sieve.

LOBSTER BUTTER 2 (Beurre de Homard)

Dry some empty cooked lobster shells in the oven, and pound them up very finely. Add an equal quantity of butter, melt in a bain-marie, stirring now and then, and pass through a sieve.

LOBSTER BUTTER 3 (American)

To four tablespoonfuls of creamed butter add three teaspoonfuls of lobster paste, half a teaspoonful of lemon juice and a dash each of paprika and dry mustard.

MAÎTRE D'HÔTEL BUTTER (Beurre Maître d'Hôtel)

Soften five ounces of butter, and add a dessertspoonful of chopped parsley, a little salt and pepper and a few drops of lemon juice.

MEUNIÈRE BUTTER (Beurre Meunière)

This is butter cooked to the noisette stage, that is until light brown and smelling of nuts, and completed with a squeeze of lemon juice and a good bunch of chopped parsley.

MINT BUTTER

To four tablespoonfuls of creamed butter add three dessertspoonfuls of very finely minced mint leaves and a teaspoonful of lemon juice. Colour the butter a delicate green.

MONTPELLIER BUTTER (Beurre de Montpellier)

Blanch some watercress, tarragon, parsley and chervil in equal quantities, as well as rather more young spinach leaves. Drain them, plunge them into cold water, and press them dry. Pound them, adding to taste chopped and blanched shallots, gherkins, capers, fillets of anchovy and a touch of garlic. To each two ounces of this purée add three hard-boiled egg yolks, salt, pepper, three quarters of a pound of butter and four dessertspoonfuls of olive oil. Pass through a sieve. The colour of this butter should be a tender green.

MUSTARD BUTTER 1 (Beurre de Moutarde)

This is softened butter to which made mustard is added in proportion according to taste or the purpose for which the butter is to be used.

MUSTARD BUTTER 2 (Hot)

Melt a quarter of a pound of butter slowly, but do not let it boil. Mix with this two teaspoonfuls of French mustard, and season with salt and pepper.

NOISETTE BUTTER (Beurre Noisette)

Cook the butter until it is a golden-brown and begins to smell like nuts.

OLIVE BUTTER

To four tablespoonfuls of creamed butter add three teaspoonfuls of olives pounded to a paste and a quarter of a teaspoonful of lemon juice.

ONION BUTTER

To four tablespoonfuls of creamed butter add a teaspoonful of onion juice.

PAPRIKA BUTTER (Beurre de Paprika)

Fry half a chopped onion in butter with a good pinch of paprika pepper. When it is cold, mix with it five ounces of softened butter and pass through a sieve.

PEANUT BUTTER

To four tablespoonfuls of peanut butter add a teaspoonful of honey, and season with salt.

PEPPER BUTTER (American)

Cream two tablespoonfuls of butter, then add a tablespoonful each of finely minced red and green sweet peppers, a crushed piece of garlic the size of a pea, a teaspoonful each of finely chopped parsley and onion, two teaspoonfuls of lemon juice, a quarter of a teaspoonful of salt and four drops of Tabasco sauce. Beat well together to mix.

Use cold with grilled steak.

PIMENTO BUTTER I (Beurre de Piment Doux)

Pound up the flesh of four small cooked sweet red peppers, then add five ounces of butter and pass through a sieve. Tinned red sweet peppers could be used, if fresh ones are not available.

PIMENTO BUTTER 2

To four tablespoonfuls of creamed butter add three dessertspoonfuls of mashed sweet red peppers and a teaspoonful of finely chopped pickles.

PISTACHIO BUTTER (Beurre aux Pistaches)

See Almond Butter (p. 181) but use blanched pistachio nuts instead of almonds.

PRAWN BUTTER

See Shrimp Butter (below), using prawns instead of shrimps.

PRINTANIER BUTTER

This is made with early season vegetables, such as carrots, French beans, peas and asparagus tips. The green vegetables are cooked quickly in boiling salted water, drained and dried, pounded with their weight in butter, and then sieved. The carrots are minced and cooked in consommé with butter and sugar until the liquid has disappeared. They are pounded, when cold, with their weight in butter, and afterwards sieved as usual.

RAVIGOTE BUTTER (Beurre Ravigote)

See Chivry Butter (p. 183).

RED HERRING BUTTER

Skin three fillets of red herrings, pound them with three ounces of butter, and pass them through a sieve.

ROQUEFORT BUTTER

With four tablespoonfuls of creamed butter mix three teaspoonfuls of Roquefort cheese.

SARDINE BUTTER I

Drain half a dozen sardines from their oil, and remove their bones and skins. Pound them with six ounces of butter, seasoning with paprika pepper, and pass through a sieve.

SARDINE BUTTER 2

To four tablespoonfuls of creamed butter add a tablespoonful of sardine paste, half a teaspoonful each of lemon and onion juice, and a dash of paprika pepper.

SHALLOT BUTTER (Beurre d'Échalote)

Blanch some chopped shallots quickly, squeeze them in a cloth, and pound them in a mortar. Mix with an equal quantity of butter, and pass through a fine sieve.

SHRIMP BUTTER (Beurre de Crevettes)

Pound shrimps with an equal weight of butter. Add a few drops of carmine and pass through a sieve.

SMOKED SALMON BUTTER (Beurre de Saumon Fumé)

Pound two ounces of smoked salmon and mix it with five ounces of butter. Pass through a sieve.

SNAIL BUTTER (Beurre pour Escargots)

This is the deliciously flavoured butter that gives snails their charm. A finely chopped shallot, a clove of garlic pounded to a paste, chopped parsley, salt and freshly ground black pepper, are mixed with butter and a liqueurglassful of good brandy. The proportion of butter to flavourings is a matter of taste but allow a good teaspoonful of the mixture per snail.

SOFT ROE BUTTER (Beurre de Laitance)

Poach some soft roes with butter and lemon juice, let them get cold, mash them to a paste, and add twice their weight of butter and a teaspoonful of made mustard for each four ounces of roe. Pass through a sieve.

TARRAGON BUTTER (Beurre d'Estragon)

Strip the tarragon leaves from their stalks, blanch them, plunge them into cold water, press them dry in a cloth, and pound them with an equal quantity of butter. Pass through a sieve.

TOMATO BUTTER (Beurre de Tomate)

This consists of very much reduced tomato pulp mixed with double its weight in butter. Pass through a sieve.

TRUFFLE BUTTER (Beurre de Truffe)

Cooked truffle is pounded with a little fish Velouté (p. 24). Add twice the amount of butter and pass through a sieve.

WHITE BUTTER (Beurre Blanc)

Reduce a good glass of white wine vinegar to which you have added a chopped shallot. Just before all the vinegar has boiled away, draw the pan from the heat and add, by degrees, half a pound of softened butter, stirring continuously. Finish with a little freshly ground pepper. Sometimes a little roughly chopped parsley is added to this butter but it should really be kept quite plain.

Sweet Sauces and Butters

These sweet sauces and butters are used to accompany steamed, boiled and baked puddings, fritters and pancakes and sometimes ice creams.

The various Hard Sauces, which are really butters, are used mostly with Christmas pudding and other similar puddings. The sauces best known are Raspberry with peaches, Melba with pears and apples and Chocolate with stewed apples, pears or bananas. Chocolate Sauce is also served, rather surprisingly, hot and separate with *Poires Hélène*, in which half a pear surmounts vanilla ice cream to receive its libation of the sauce – an admirable combination.

ALBERT SAUCE

To a pint of hot Custard (p. 200), add at the last minute a teaspoonful of brandy or liqueur, and one or two spoonfuls of finely shredded candied peel, previously marinated in a little liqueur syrup.

ALMOND SAUCE I

½ tbs. arrowroot; 1 pint milk; 1 tbs. sugar; 4 oz. ground almonds; almond essence.

Mix the arrowroot smoothly with a little of the milk, then add the rest and bring to the boil. As soon as the mixture thickens, add the sugar and ground almonds. Stir and cook for three or four minutes, then add three or four drops of almond essence and let the sauce get cold.

ALMOND SAUCE 2

Blanch and skin an ounce of Jordan almonds and three bitter almonds. Pound them in a mortar with a little orange-flower water. Put this into a saucepan with a quarter of a pint of cream and the yolks of two eggs, and whisk over a low heat until thick.

Sweet Sauces and Butters

APPLE SAUCE

Make some Apple Sauce in the usual way (p. 43), but use brown sugar instead of white, and add powdered mace, cinnamon and grated lemon rind to your taste.

APRICOT SAUCE 1

fresh apricots; Madeira; Demerara sugar.

Cut fresh apricots in halves, crack their stones, peel and pound the kernels and add them to the fruit in a saucepan with a little water. Stew them over a gentle heat until the fruit is quite soft, then add a glass of Madeira for each dozen apricots and sweeten with Demerara sugar. Stir well and reduce until the sauce is syrupy, then pass through a sieve and serve hot.

APRICOT SAUCE 2

Mix together two tablespoonfuls of apricot jam, two ounces of sugar and a glass of white wine, and warm for five minutes over the heat.

APRICOT SAUCE 3 (American)

Rub some tinned or stewed dried apricots through a sieve, adding sugar if necessary. Then fold the purée into an equal amount of whipped double cream.

ARROWROOT SAUCE

cinnamon stick, lemon rind or other flavouring; ½ pint cider; 1 level dessertsp. arrowroot; sugar.

Simmer a piece of cinnamon stick, lemon rind or other flavouring in half a pint of cider for ten minutes. Mix the arrowroot smoothly with a little water and strain the cider into it, stirring all the time. Add sugar to taste, and simmer for about five minutes. Equal parts of wine and water, or any sort of fruit juice, can be substituted for the cider if preferred.

BANANA SAUCE 1

2 ripe bananas; lemon peel; 1½ oz. sugar; ¼ pint sherry.
Peel the bananas and rub them through a sieve. Put half a pint of

water into a saucepan with a strip of lemon peel and the sugar, and bring to the boil. Add the banana purée and boil for ten minutes, then add the sherry and bring to the boil again. Strain before serving.

BANANA SAUCE 2

3 level tsp. butter; 3 level tsp. flour; 4 tbs. sugar; 8 tbs. milk; 1 egg yolk; 1 ripe banana; salt; ¼ pint double cream.

Cream the butter and blend it with the flour, then cream with the sugar. Scald the milk, add the mixture to it, and stir until it thickens. Now add the slightly beaten egg yolk, and cook on for three minutes, still stirring, then add the skinned and sieved banana. Chill this sauce, and finish with a few grains of salt and the double cream, stiffly whisked.

BANANA NUT MAYONNAISE SAUCE (American)

Mash a small ripe banana with three dessertspoonfuls of peanut butter, and combine them with eight to ten tablespoonfuls of Mayonnaise Sauce (p. 28). Thin down, if necessary, with a little cream.

BEETROOT SAUCE (Rose Sauce)

1 small cooked beetroot; 1 small lemon; ½ lb. sugar; ¼ tsp. vanilla essence.

Peel the beetroot and cut it in slices, and then boil these in half a pint of cold water with the lemon rind for half an hour. Strain off the liquid and put it back into the pan with the sugar, the juice of the lemon and vanilla essence. Boil for another five minutes and serve hot or cold.

Use with steamed puddings or moulds.

BERRY SAUCE (American)

Crushed and sweetened fresh strawberries, raspberries or blackberries are folded into an equal amount of fresh whipped cream.

BISCHOFF SAUCE

8 fl. oz. white wine; sugar; ½ orange; ½ lemon; 3 tbs. raisins; 1 tbs. shredded almonds; 1 tbs. shredded candied peel.

Put the white wine into a saucepan with the same amount of hot water and sugar to taste. Add the coloured skin only of half an orange and half a lemon, bring just to the boil, take off the heat and remove the orange and lemon peel. Now add the seeded raisins, shredded almonds and finely shredded candied peel. Cover and leave for half an hour, bringing just to the boil before serving.

Use with Cabinet or similar pudding.

BRANDY BUTTER

Beat a quarter of a pound of butter with a wooden spoon until it looks like cream, then add a quarter of a pound of fine castor sugar, or rather less, and then by small degrees a glass of sherry and a small glass of brandy.

BRANDY SAUCE I

3 egg yolks; ¼ pint cream; 1 dessertsp. Demerara sugar; 1 wineglass good brandy.

Mix the egg yolks with the cream, add the Demerara sugar and the brandy. Beat well together and warm up in a double saucepan or in a bain-marie for about ten minutes, stirring all the time.

BRANDY SAUCE 2

Melt an ounce and a half of fresh butter and add to it an egg yolk, mixing well for some minutes in a basin. Then add two spoonfuls of sifted sugar and pour in two or three spoonfuls of brandy *very gradually.*

Use with Christmas pudding.

BRANDY SAUCE 3 (Swiss)

Warm two ounces of fresh butter with a tablespoonful of castor sugar until both are melted. Then add a glass of Madeira and a small glass of brandy and serve warm.

Use with Christmas pudding.

BRANDY CUSTARD SAUCE

Strain three egg yolks into nearly half a pint of warm milk in which an ounce of sugar has been dissolved. Cook in a double saucepan until thick, and then add a spoonful of brandy.

BROWN SAUCE

Make some Melted-Butter Sauce (p. 96) with a brown roux (p. 25), moistening it with milk flavoured to taste with caramel (p. 36) and powdered cinnamon. Add a well-beaten egg and a spoonful or two of brandy at the last.

Use with steamed puddings.

BUTTERSCOTCH SAUCE

6 oz. moist brown sugar; ¼ pint corn syrup; 1½ oz. butter; ¼ pint cream; ¼ tsp. vanilla essence.

Put into a saucepan the brown sugar, corn syrup, an eighth of a pint of water and the butter, and stir and cook over a low heat until the sugar is dissolved. Then cook on to the soft-ball stage (245°F.). Take the pan off the heat, and stir in by degrees the cream and vanilla essence. This sauce is served hot or cold.

BUTTERSCOTCH ALMOND SAUCE

Add chopped almonds to Butterscotch Sauce above.

CAMBRIDGE SAUCE

2 oz. butter; 6 oz. sugar; 2 level tsp. flour; 1 tsp. vanilla essence.

Cream the butter with the sugar. Mix the flour with five teaspoonfuls of cold water, add gradually a quarter of a pint of boiling water and boil for five minutes. Let this cool, and just before serving mix it with the creamed butter and sugar and add the vanilla essence.

CARAMEL SAUCE I

1 oz. lump sugar; ½ lemon; ½ pint sugar syrup; 1 dessertsp. cornflour; vanilla.

Boil the lump sugar with the juice of half a lemon until a light golden colour, then add the sugar syrup (that is, a quarter of a pound of sugar boiled with half a pint of water and reduced to half a pint in all). Boil on until smooth, then thicken with the cornflour mixed with a little water, and when the sauce is thick flavour with a little vanilla and strain if necessary.

CARAMEL SAUCE 2

6 oz. sugar; ½ lemon; cinnamon; 4 tbs. castor sugar; 1 glass Madeira or ½ glass brandy.

Put a pint of cold water into a saucepan with the ordinary sugar, the yellow part of the rind of half a lemon and a little cinnamon. Bring it gradually to the boil and simmer for ten minutes. Meanwhile put the castor sugar into another saucepan with a little water and stir it continuously over the heat with a wooden spoon until the water disappears and the sugar begins to brown. Then add the contents of the other saucepan after passing them through a fine sieve. Add the Madeira or brandy, stir well together and serve hot.

CARAMEL SAUCE 3

Put six ounces of sugar in a thick metal saucepan, and melt it over a moderate heat with a small squeeze of lemon, stirring all the while, until it is a light brown. Then add slowly two tablespoonfuls of clear coffee and six of water, and boil for six minutes.

CHANTILLY APPLE SAUCE

1 lb. cooking apples; 1 oz. butter; 1½ oz. castor sugar; ¼ pint double cream.

Peel, core and slice the apples, and put them into a stewpan with two or three tablespoonfuls of water, the butter and castor sugar. Stew until tender, then pass through a fine sieve. Whip the cream stiffly, and stir it into the apple purée.

CHAUDEAU SAUCE I

3 oz. sugar; 3 eggs; juice of 1 orange or lemon; ½ pint sweet white wine; 1 tbs. maraschino.

Cream the sugar with the eggs and the orange or lemon juice. Beat until frothy, then put into a double saucepan, and add the sweet white wine and maraschino. Heat up without boiling, stirring all the time, then take off the heat, and beat for two or three minutes before serving.

CHAUDEAU SAUCE 2

Put two yolks of eggs, half a wineglassful each of sherry and water and half a tablespoonful of castor sugar into a saucepan, and whisk them well by the side of the heat until the mixture is thick and frothy.

CHERRY SAUCE 1

1 tbs. cornflour; ½ pint cherry juice; 1 tbs. lemon juice; 2 oz. fresh butter; 6 oz. castor sugar; cinnamon.

Mix the cornflour with a quarter of a pint of water until smooth, then add the cherry juice and the lemon juice and bring to the boil, cooking for ten minutes and stirring well. Then add the butter, castor sugar and a pinch of cinnamon. Stir well to mix.

Use with pancakes, fritters or any other suitable sweet.

CHERRY SAUCE 2

½ lb. cherries; ¼ pint red wine; 1 tbs. sugar; cinnamon; lemon rind; 1 dessertsp. arrowroot.

Stone the cherries, crack the stones and put the kernels with the fruit. Pound these together and put them into a saucepan with a quarter of a pint of water, the red wine, sugar, a little cinnamon and a piece of lemon rind. Boil until the cherries are cooked, then rub them through a sieve. Thicken this sauce with the arrowroot mixed smoothly with a little cold water. If you like, before serving, warm up in the sauce a few fresh stoned cherries, whole or halved.

CHERRY SAUCE 3

¼lb. sugar; 1 dessertsp. red-currant jelly; ½ lemon; ½ small glass port wine; 1 oz. glacé cherries.

Boil the sugar in half a pint of water in a small saucepan and reduce to half a pint in all. Add the red-currant jelly, the juice of half a lemon and the port wine. Simmer until the jelly is dissolved, then add the halved or quartered glacé cherries, bring to the boil, skim and serve.

CHERRY SAUCE 4

Reduce the syrup of some stewed cherries by half, add to it an equal quantity of red-currant jelly, and flavour with Kirsch.

CHOCOLATE SAUCE 1

The best and really only Chocolate Sauce is made simply by dissolving plain sweet chocolate with a very little water, sweetening and flavouring it as desired, and finishing it with cream and small pieces of butter.

CHOCOLATE SAUCE 2

Dissolve half an ounce of grated chocolate in half a pint of milk and add half a teaspoonful of vanilla essence. Make a roux with half an ounce of butter and the same of flour, add the milk, and stir until the sauce cooks and thickens.

CHOCOLATE SAUCE 3 (Swedish)

3 oz. cocoa powder; 3 tsp. potato flour; sugar; ¼ pint double cream.

Boil a scant pint of water, add the cocoa powder, whisking well, and then the potato flour mixed smoothly with a little water. Boil for two minutes until the sauce thickens, then add sugar to taste and presently mix the sauce with the cream stiffly whipped. Serve cold.

CHOCOLATE SAUCE 4

4 oz. sugar; 4 oz. unsweetened chocolate; ½ tsp. vanilla essence; 4 fl. oz. cream.

Put the sugar and eight tablespoonfuls of water into a saucepan and boil for five minutes. Let this syrup cook and then stir into it slowly the melted unsweetened chocolate and the vanilla essence. Keep the sauce in a double saucepan until wanted, and at the last moment add the cream.

CHOCOLATE SAUCE 5

1 dessertsp. butter; 3 egg yolks; 5 oz. plain grated chocolate; 1 pint milk; sugar.

Cream a dessertspoonful of butter and add the beaten egg yolks. Put this into a double saucepan and add the chocolate. Heat slowly while the chocolate melts, but do not allow it to boil. Now bring a pint of milk to the boil, add it to the chocolate mixture and heat until the sauce thickens. Add sugar to taste after removing the pan from the heat.

CHOCOLATE SAUCE 6

Dissolve half a pound of grated plain chocolate in two thirds of a pint of water. Add a tablespoonful of vanilla sugar, cook gently for twenty-five minutes, and complete at the last minute with three tablespoonfuls of cream and a piece of fresh butter, the size of a walnut.

Note on Chocolate Sauces

A discreet touch of cinnamon is nearly always an improvement to Chocolate Sauces, as is the addition of a little strong black coffee, which seems to enhance the flavour of the chocolate. In the same way, the addition of a very little chocolate to a Coffee Sauce seems to bring out the flavour of the coffee.

CHOCOLATE FUDGE SAUCE

5 oz. cocoa powder; 6 oz. sugar; ½ level tsp. salt; 3 level tsp. cornflour; 6 tbs. white corn syrup; 8 tbs. milk; 3 level dessertsp. butter; 2 tsp. vanilla essence.

Mix together the cocoa powder, sugar, salt, and cornflour, and add the white corn syrup and milk. Cook for a quarter of an hour in a double saucepan, and when it thickens, add the butter, and after it has cooled, the vanilla essence.

CIDER SAUCE

½ tbs. arrowroot or potato flour; 1 pint cider; sugar; 3 tbs. lemon juice; ¼ lb. sultanas; powdered cloves.

Make a smooth paste with the arrowroot or potato flour and a little of the cider, and then add the rest of the cider, sugar to taste, lemon juice, sultanas and a pinch of powdered cloves. Bring to the boil and stir until smooth. Serve hot or cold.

CINNAMON SAUCE (Dutch)

1 oz. flour; 2 oz. sugar; ½ pint milk; cinnamon stick.

Mix the flour with the sugar and moisten with a little of the cold milk. Put the rest of the milk into a saucepan with a stick of cinnamon, bring to the boil and simmer until the milk is well flavoured. Then stir in the flour and sugar, and simmer for five minutes, stirring all the time. Take out the cinnamon stick before serving.

COCONUT SAUCE

Add to a Hard Sauce (p. 203), the yolks of two eggs, and when it is very light and creamy, add the whisked whites and ten tablespoonfuls of grated coconut.

COFFEE SAUCE I

Make a white roux (p. 23) with half an ounce of butter and the same of flour, and moisten with a quarter of a pint of milk mixed with a quarter of a pint of strong good coffee. Stir until the sauce cooks and thickens, sweeten to taste and add a little vanilla essence.

COFFEE SAUCE 2 (Austrian)

Mix about a quarter of a pint of strong clear coffee with three quarters of a pint of rich Custard (p. 200), and stir together in a bain-marie until nearly but not quite boiling. Then stir in an eighth of a pint of thick cream, and the same of maraschino. Serve hot.

COFFEE CREAM SAUCE

3 level tbs. sugar; 8 egg yolks; ⅛ tsp. salt; 1½ pints strong coffee; 3 fl. oz. double cream.

Add the sugar to the slightly beaten egg yolks with the salt, and then gradually add the coffee. Cook in a double saucepan until thick, then cool, and fold in the cream, stiffly whisked.

CORNFLOUR SAUCE

½ pint milk; 1 lemon; 1 level dessertsp. cornflour; 1 level dessertsp. sugar.

Infuse the milk with the finely-peeled rind of the lemon for five minutes, then mix the cornflour with a little cold milk, and strain the lemon-flavoured milk onto it, stirring all the time. Sweeten with the sugar and boil for one minute before serving.

CRANBERRY SAUCE

1 pint fresh or frozen cranberries; 2 oz. castor sugar; 1 tbs. red-currant jelly; ½ glass port (optional).

Put the washed cranberries into a saucepan with a quarter of a pint of water, bring to the boil, and simmer quietly for half an hour. Then add the sugar, red-currant jelly and, if you like, half a glass of port. Bring to the boil again, and strain before serving, hot or cold.

CURRANT JELLY SAUCE

This is simply red-currant jelly melted and thickened with a little arrowroot, a little lemon juice being added.

CUSTARD SAUCE

1 pint milk; 1 bayleaf; 3 oz. castor sugar; 2 eggs; 1 tbs. brandy.

Bring the milk to the boil with the bayleaf in it, add the castor sugar, and let it cool slightly. Beat up the eggs, pour the milk onto them, and strain into a jug. Put the jug into a saucepan of boiling water, stir the Custard until it thickens, being careful to see that it does not boil, and finish with the brandy. (Both bayleaf and brandy may be omitted, if desired. Vanilla is now more commonly used for flavouring: add one teaspoonful if using essence.)

DEARBORN SAUCE

4 oz. butter; 6 oz. brown sugar; cream; sherry; brandy.

Cream the butter and brown sugar, then add three dessertspoonfuls of cream and four teaspoonfuls of sherry, drop by drop, and three dessertspoonfuls of brandy. Finish with a small pinch of salt.

DENVER SAUCE

Make like Hard Sauce with Cream (p. 203), using two ounces of butter, eight ounces of icing sugar, three dessertspoonfuls of strong coffee, two level teaspoonfuls of cocoa and a teaspoonful of vanilla essence.

DEWEY SAUCE 1

Bring eight ounces of sugar and four tablespoonfuls of red fruit juice to the boil, and boil to a thin syrup. Pour this slowly onto two well-beaten egg yolks, and cook until it thickens slightly, stirring all the time. Red colouring can be added, if thought necessary.

DEWEY SAUCE 2

Make the sauce as above, using water instead of fruit juice, and flavouring it with two tablespoonfuls of rum and a teaspoonful of Curaçao.

ENGLISH SAUCE

This is the same as an ordinary Custard Sauce (p. 200).

FLORODORA SAUCE

1 egg; 6 oz. icing sugar; 6 fl. oz. cream; ½ tsp. vanilla essence; salt; Madeira (optional).

Stiffly beat the egg white and, beating all the while and by small degrees, add the icing sugar. Then add the thickly beaten egg yolk, stiffly beaten cream, vanilla essence and a small pinch of salt. A further flavouring of Madeira can be added, if liked.

FROTHED SAUCE

Whisk together over boiling water a wineglassful of sherry, a third of that amount of warm water, two tablespoonfuls of fine white sugar and two yolks of eggs. At the last moment add three stiffly whisked egg whites, and warm through to serve.

FRUIT JUICE SAUCE

Mix three level teaspoonfuls of cornflour with eight ounces of sugar, add eight tablespoonfuls of boiling water, and boil for five minutes. When cool, add about four ounces of the chosen fruit juice, fresh or tinned, and three dessertspoonfuls of lemon juice.

FRUIT SYRUP SAUCE (Swedish)

6 tbs. sweet fruit syrup; 1 tbs. potato flour; lemon juice.

Bring the fruit syrup to the boil with three quarters of a pint of water and while it is boiling add the potato flour mixed with a little cold water, and boil for two minutes longer. Add more sweetening, if necessary, and lemon juice to taste. Serve hot or cold.

GINGER SAUCE

Boil together half a pint of water, a quarter of a pound of sugar and the juice of a lemon until you have a syrup (about ten minutes); then add an ounce of shredded preserved ginger, bring to the boil again, and serve.

GINGER SYRUP SAUCE

Take about a quarter of a pint of the syrup from a jar of stem ginger, add a little butter and a few lumps of sugar rubbed on the rind of orange or lemon, and heat up and serve with a suitable steamed pudding.

GOLDEN SYRUP SAUCE

2 tbs. golden syrup; 2 tsp. lemon juice; 1 tsp. cornflour.

Put the golden syrup into a saucepan with four tablespoonfuls of water and the lemon juice. Mix the cornflour with a little cold water, bring the syrup to the boil, and add the cornflour to it. Simmer until the sauce is slightly thick, stirring all the time.

GOOSEBERRY SAUCE

Stew half a pound of green gooseberries with very little water until they are soft, then pass them through a fine sieve. Add sugar to taste and then mix with half a pint of hot White Sauce (p. 24) made with milk.

Use with milk puddings.

GUAVA SAUCE

Peel fresh, cooked or tinned guavas and mash to a smooth seedless pulp. Mix this with sugar alone, or also with lemon or lime juice or mixed spice. If liked, the white of an egg may be whisked in. Serve like Apple Sauce.

HARD SAUCE

4 good tbs. butter; 10 level tbs. castor sugar; nutmeg; ½ tsp. vanilla essence or lemon juice or 1 tbs. brandy or rum.

Cream the butter, gradually add the castor sugar, and beat until the mixture is smooth. Then add a suspicion of nutmeg and flavour either with the vanilla essence or lemon juice or with the brandy or rum, according to taste. These must be added very slowly, beating all the time. Keep on ice or in a cold place to harden.

HARD SAUCE WITH CREAM

Add a quarter of a pint of double cream, drop by drop, to ordinary Hard Sauce, beating well all the while.

Hard Sauce Variations (Sweet Butters)

Brandy Butter	New Forest Sauce
Coconut Sauce	Ohio Sauce
Dearborn Sauce	Senior Wrangler Sauce
Denver Sauce	

HAZEL-NUT SAUCE

Custard (p. 200); 2 oz. hazel-nuts; pralin; sugar; almonds.
Flavour an English Custard with an infusion of grilled hazel-nuts (three to four strained tablespoons in all), and add one tablespoonful of moulded filbert pralin per pint of Custard. This is a sauce from Escoffier, who gives a recipe for the pralin, as follows: 'Gently melt one pound of powdered sugar in a small saucepan, taking care not to let it acquire a deeper shade than old gold. Mix twenty ounces of dried almonds with it; turn the whole out onto the corner of a slightly-oiled marble slab (or an over-turned saucepan lid), and leave it to cool.

When the nougat is quite cold, pound it and rub it through a sieve. . . . Put the powder in a well-closed box, and place the latter in a dry place.'

HONEY SAUCE

Mix smoothly two level teaspoonfuls of cornflour with three dessert-spoonfuls of melted butter, then add six tablespoonfuls of honey, and cook for five minutes.

HONEY CREAM SAUCE

Whip three fl. ounces of double cream until thick, then add three tablespoonfuls of honey and a teaspoonful of lemon juice. Whip all the time, until well mixed.

HONEY CREAM MAYONNAISE SAUCE (American)

Mix smoothly together a quarter of a level teaspoonful of dry mustard, three teaspoonfuls of honey and half a teaspoonful of lemon juice. Add to six tablespoonfuls of Mayonnaise Sauce (p. 28), season with salt, and then fold in four tablespoonfuls of whipped double cream.

Use with fruit salads.

JAM SAUCE I

1 tbs. jam; 1 tbs. sugar; lemon juice; ½ tsp. cornflour.

Boil together a quarter of a pint of water, the jam, sugar and a little lemon juice. Add the cornflour mixed smoothly with a little water, and boil up again, stirring, until the sauce thickens.

JAM SAUCE 2

Boil together for a few minutes a teacupful each of jam, sugar and water and the juice of half a lemon. Then strain and serve.

JAM SAUCE 3

2 tbs. jam; 1 liqueurglass Kirsch, brandy or rum.

Dilute the jam with a quarter of a pint of hot water and the Kirsch, brandy or rum, according to the sort of jam used. Stir well over the heat so as to moisten the jam thoroughly, then strain into a hot sauce-boat. For strawberry or raspberry jam sauce a squeeze of lemon as a finishing touch is an improvement.

JELLY SAUCE

Stir half a glassful of any fruit jelly until it is smooth and then beat into it lightly the whisked whites of two eggs.

KIRSCH SAUCE

Dissolve four ounces of white sugar in about a pint of water, bring to the boil, and when it boils, add slowly half a tablespoonful of arrowroot or cornflour previously mixed smoothly with a little cold water. Stir until clear, then add one tablespoonful or so of Kirsch.

LEMON SAUCE I

Rub all the rind off a large lemon on lump sugar; pound the sugar and add the strained juice of the lemon. Add more sugar, making half a pound in all. Boil it, adding a piece of butter rolled in flour.

LEMON SAUCE 2

1 lemon; $\frac{1}{2}$ pint milk; sugar; $\frac{1}{2}$ oz. butter; $\frac{1}{2}$ oz. flour.

Infuse the thinly cut rind of the lemon in the milk, then make a sauce with the strained milk, sugar to taste, and a white roux (p. 23) made with the butter and flour. When the sauce is cooked, add the juice of half of the lemon, but be careful not to heat up the sauce after doing this, or it will curdle.

LEMON SAUCE 3

1 large lemon; 1–2 oz. sugar; 1 oz. butter; 2 eggs.

Peel the rind of the lemon very thinly, and boil it in a quarter of a pint of water for five minutes. Then add the sugar, butter, the lemon juice and beaten eggs. Stir very carefully over a gentle heat until the mixture thickens, then strain it and serve.

LEMON SAUCE 4

Boil six ounces of sugar with three dessertspoonfuls of light corn syrup and four tablespoonfuls of water for five minutes. Then take off the heat, and finish with two level teaspoonfuls of butter in small pieces and three of lemon juice.

LEMON SAUCE 5

4 oz. sugar; 3 level tsp. cornflour; 3 level dessertsp. butter; 4½ tsp. lemon juice; salt; nutmeg.

Mix together the sugar and cornflour, add gradually half a pint of boiling water, and boil for five minutes. Then take off the heat and add the butter, lemon juice, a tiny pinch of salt and a little grated nutmeg.

LIME SAUCE

4 tbs. sugar; 2 limes; liqueur, brandy or rum.

Put the sugar into a saucepan with half a pint of water, and the very finely peeled rind of a lime, simmer for twenty minutes, add the juice of two limes and a liqueurglassful of any liqueur, brandy or rum, then strain and serve. A drop or two of cochineal will improve the colour of the sauce.

MAPLE CREAM SAUCE

Boil ten ounces of maple syrup with four tablespoonfuls of cream to the soft-ball stage (245°F.), beat for one minute and serve as it is, or with three tablespoonfuls of chopped nuts added to it.

MAPLE FOAM SAUCE (Canadian)

Beat the yolks of two eggs in a basin and then add two whole eggs well beaten, five ounces of maple syrup, the same of water, and a large wineglassful of sherry. Put the basin in a pan of hot water, and cook very slowly, whisking continuously to make the sauce foamy.

MAPLE NUT SAUCE (American)

Boil one pint of maple syrup with an ounce of butter to a very soft-ball stage (245°F.), then add six tablespoonfuls of chopped nuts and serve hot or cold.

MAPLE SUGAR SAUCE

Cook one pint of maple sugar with eight tablespoonfuls of cream until the mixture bubbles, then add three level teaspoonfuls of butter and two teaspoonfuls of vanilla essence, and beat until the sauce is thick.

MARASCHINO CHERRY SAUCE

2 tbs. cornflour; 3 oz. sugar; 3 tbs. Maraschino cherries; butter; 4 tbs. syrup from cherries.

Mix together the cornflour and sugar, and add them, stirring all the time, to six fl. ounces of boiling water. Boil for five minutes, and then add the Maraschino cherries cut in halves, not quite a dessert-spoonful of butter, and the syrup from the cherries.

MARMALADE SAUCE I

1 tbs. marmalade; ½ lemon; ½ tsp. cornflour; ½ oz. sugar; sherry or orange-flavoured liqueur.

Boil the marmalade with a quarter of a pint of water and the thinly cut rind of half a lemon. Thicken with the cornflour mixed with a little water, adding the sugar and the juice of the lemon-half. Serve as it is, or strain. A little sherry or orange-flavoured liqueur may be added, with great advantage, at the last moment.

MARMALADE SAUCE 2

Put one pound of orange marmalade into a saucepan with two wineglassfuls of white wine. Stir over a gentle heat until very hot, then strain.

MARMALADE MAYONNAISE SAUCE (American)

To six tablespoonfuls of Mayonnaise Sauce (p. 28) add two table-spoonfuls of orange marmalade.

Use with fruit salad.

MARSHMALLOW SAUCE

Cut four ounces of marshmallows into pieces with a pair of scissors, and melt them in a double saucepan. Dissolve ten ounces of icing sugar in three tablespoonfuls of boiling water, add this to the marshmallows, and stir until well mixed.

MARSHMALLOW MINT SAUCE

4 oz. sugar; 8 marshmallows; 1 egg white; oil of peppermint.

Boil the sugar with four tablespoonfuls of water for five minutes, then add the marshmallows cut in small pieces. Beat the egg white stiffly and add the first mixture gradually to it. Flavour with a drop of oil of peppermint and colour green. Then chill.

MELBA SAUCE I (American)

Crush one pound of fresh or tinned raspberries, sieve finely, add two tablespoonfuls of sugar, and cook to a thick syrup.

(This actually approximates to the garnish for Escoffier's original *Pêche Melba*, which is simply designated as a raspberry purée.)

MELBA SAUCE 2 (American)

1 lb. raspberries; 6 tbs. red-currant jelly; 4 oz. sugar; arrowroot or cornflour.

Mix together the sieved raspberries with their juice, the red-currant jelly and the sugar. Bring to the boil, and when the jelly is quite melted, thicken with a level teaspoonful and a half of arrowroot or cornflour mixed smoothly with three teaspoonfuls of cold water. Strain and cool.

MIDDLETON SAUCE

Mix the yolks of four eggs with half a pint of single cream, and cook as a Custard (p. 200); add a little grated lemon peel and a glass of sherry made hot, and whisk all to a froth.

MINCEMEAT SAUCE

Boil eight tablespoonfuls of water with four ounces of sugar for five minutes and then add about one pound of mincemeat.

MOCK MAPLE SAUCE

Dissolve six ounces of moist sugar in six tablespoonfuls of water, add a pinch of salt, and boil for one minute. Add a quarter of a teaspoonful of vanilla essence and serve hot or cold.

MOLASSES SAUCE

Boil half a pint of molasses with four and a half level teaspoonfuls of butter for five minutes, then take off the heat, and add three dessertspoonfuls of lemon juice.

NEW FOREST SAUCE

¼ *lb. fresh butter; ¼ lb. castor sugar; 1 tbs. brandy; 2 tbs. sherry; nutmeg.*

Beat up the butter and castor sugar until white and light over a pan of hot water. Add the brandy and sherry by slow degrees with a very little nutmeg, and beat all together until thoroughly mixed. Serve in a sauce-boat.

Use particularly with Christmas Pudding.

NOISETTE SAUCE

This is an ordinary Custard Sauce (p. 200) to which crushed hazel-nut pralin (p. 203) has been added. It is extraordinarily good.

OHIO SAUCE

Make this like Hard Sauce with Cream (p. 203), using four ounces of butter, six ounces of brown sugar, three tablespoonfuls of cream, half a teaspoonful of lemon essence, and at the end, three level dessertspoonfuls each of chopped dates and nuts.

ORANGE SAUCE 1

Cream a cup of sugar with half a cup of butter and blend in a cup of orange juice.

ORANGE SAUCE 2 (Swedish)

3 eggs; 4 oz. sugar; 2 oranges; 1 lemon; ½ pint double cream.

Beat the egg yolks with half of the sugar for twenty minutes. Then beat the egg whites stiffly and mix them with the remaining sugar. Combine the two mixtures, adding the juice of the oranges and the grated peel and juice of the lemon. Finally stir in the double cream stiffly whipped and serve at once.

ORANGE SAUCE 3

A mixture of two thirds orange marmalade and a third apricot purée or jam. Flavour with Curaçao.

ORANGE SAUCE 4 (American)

Beat three egg whites until stiff, then add gradually half a pound or so of icing sugar, and go on beating. Finally add the grated rind and juice of two oranges and the juice of one lemon.

ORANGE SYRUP SAUCE

Just cover two ounces of sugar with cold water, and boil it until it is clear, skimming all the time. Then add the strained juice of six oranges and, if liked, a few drops of lemon juice. Skim again well, and use hot or cold.

PEAR SAUCE

Make exactly as Apple Sauce (p. 43), but using pears instead, and flavouring it with spice, lemon or ginger.

PINEAPPLE SAUCE

Chop up finely some fresh or tinned pineapple, sweeten according to your taste, and thicken with arrowroot.

PINEAPPLE MINT SAUCE

Simmer a breakfastcupful of crushed pineapple with the same quantity of sugar and three quarters of a breakfastcupful of water for ten minutes. Then let it cool, and colour it green, after adding six drops of oil of peppermint. This sauce should be served chilled.

PLUM PUDDING SAUCE

1 oz. butter; 1 tbs. castor sugar; 1 small glass brandy or rum; 1 small glass Madeira.

Put the butter and castor sugar into a basin, and leave it on the stove until the butter melts. Now stir in the brandy or rum and the Madeira with a quarter of a pint of water, adding more sugar if it is not sweet enough. Stir together, and when the sauce is hot enough to use, pour it over the pudding or hand it in a sauce-boat.

PORT WINE SAUCE

See Wine Sauce (p. 217), but use port wine instead of white wine, increase the sugar a little, and add a dessertspoonful of lemon juice and a grating of nutmeg.

PRUNE SAUCE (Scandinavian)

½ lb. prunes; 2 tbs. sugar.

Soak the prunes in one and a half pints of water overnight, then bring them to the boil in the same water, adding the sugar and cooking on until the prunes fall to pieces. Pass all through a sieve and dilute with more water if necessary. This sauce can be served either hot or cold.

PUNCH SAUCE (Swiss)

1 tsp. potato flour; 2 glasses red wine; 1 lemon; mixed spice; sugar; 1 small glass brandy.

Mix the potato flour with a little water out of a glassful, then add the rest of the water, the red wine, the juice of a lemon and a pinch of mixed spice. Bring to the boil and cook for a minute or two; then add sugar to taste, strain the sauce when this is dissolved, and finally add the brandy.

Use hot with fritters.

QUINCE SAUCE

Make as Apple Sauce (p. 43), but using ripe quinces and flavouring it with lemon. Half apples, half quinces may be used if preferred, as the flavour of the quinces alone may be too astringent and too perfumed for many.

RAISIN SAUCE

Simmer a breakfastcupful of seeded or seedless raisins, chopped finely, in a breakfastcupful and a half of water, until they are soft. Then add four ounces of sugar, and continue cooking slowly for a quarter of an hour. Lastly, add four teaspoonfuls of lemon juice.

RAISIN AND CURRANT SAUCE (American)

1½ lb. currants; ¾ lb. brown sugar; ¾ lb. raisins.

Stem and mash the ripe currants and add the brown sugar. Bring slowly to the boil, skimming, then add the seeded raisins. Cook on together until the raisins are thoroughly soft, removing any scum that rises and stirring after each skimming. Serve the sauce when it is cool.

RASPBERRY SAUCE 1

Melt some raspberry jelly, thicken it with arrowroot, and flavour it with Kirsch.

RASPBERRY SAUCE 2

See Strawberry Sauce (p. 215) and use raspberries instead.

RED-CURRANT JELLY SAUCE (American)

Beat three quarters of a pound of red-currant jelly with a fork until it is light, then add the rind of a quarter of an orange cut in very thin strips, and one tablespoonful of lemon juice.

REGENT SAUCE

This is a syrup made of a glass of white wine, the grated rind and strained juice of half a lemon, and two ounces of sugar.

ROSE SAUCE

See Beetroot Sauce (p. 192).

ROXBURY SAUCE

1 egg; ¾ lb. icing sugar; 1 level tsp. cornflour; ⅛ level tsp. salt; 8 tbs. scalded milk; ½ tsp. vanilla essence; lemon rind and juice.

Beat an egg yolk thickly, and beat into it two thirds of the icing sugar. Mix the remaining sugar with the cornflour and salt, and pour onto this, by degrees, the scalded milk. Cook until thick in a double saucepan, add the egg mixture to it, flavour with the vanilla essence, three teaspoonfuls of lemon juice and the grated rind of a quarter of a lemon, and lastly add the stiffly beaten egg white.

RUM SAUCE

egg yolks; sugar; milk; double cream; rum.

Make a Custard with the yolks of three eggs (no whites), a teaspoonful of sugar, two tablespoonfuls of milk, one tablespoonful of cream, one teaspoonful of rum. Whip all over the fire in a bain-marie pan in hot water until thick. Then put in a cool place to get quite cold and set. Whip half a pint of cream to a stiff froth, adding gradually a tablespoonful of rum and a dessertspoonful of sugar. Add this to the cold Custard and put it into the refrigerator for twenty minutes before serving.

RUM EGG SAUCE

1 small wineglass rum; 2 eggs; 1½ oz. castor sugar.

Put the rum into a saucepan with the eggs and castor sugar, and an eighth of a pint of water; stand the pan in a larger one containing boiling water, and whisk well until the sauce is thick and frothy. Brandy can be substituted for rum.

Use especially for Christmas Pudding.

SABAYON SAUCE 1

3 egg yolks; 2 oz. castor sugar; ¼ lemon; ¼ glass Marsala; ¼ glass sweet white wine.

Put into a basin the egg yolks, castor sugar, the grated rind of a quarter of a lemon, and the Marsala and sweet white wine. Put the basin over a pan of hot water and beat the contents gently until they make three or four times the original quantity. Be careful to see that the sauce does not approach boiling point.

SABAYON SAUCE 2

¼ lb. icing sugar; 4 egg yolks; ½ pint dry white wine.

Mix the icing sugar with the egg yolks until the mixture has whitened slightly, then dilute with the dry white wine and whisk in a narrow pan over another of boiling water, until it is four times its original size, and firm and frothy. This sauce can also be made with milk instead of white wine and then flavoured according to choice.

SAGO SAUCE

1 tbs. large sago; lemon rind and juice; 1 small glass sherry.

Bring a third of a pint of water to the boil and add the sago and a few thin strips of lemon rind. Simmer gently until the sago is quite clear, then take out the lemon rind, add the sherry and a dessertspoonful of lemon juice, sweeten to taste, heat up well and serve.

SAUCE BELGE

2 oz. sugar; ½ tsp. cinnamon; nutmeg; 1 dessertsp. cornflour; 2 oz. butter.

Put the sugar, powdered cinnamon, a pinch of nutmeg and cornflour into a saucepan, and mix smoothly with a little cold water. Then add half a pint of boiling water and simmer for about ten minutes, stirring it well. Finish with the butter.

Use with boiled or steamed puddings.

SAUCE DIPLOMATE

Boil together a quarter of a pound of lump sugar and half a pint of water for a quarter of an hour, then thicken with a little potato flour. Stir in at the last a wineglassful of claret and the juice of half a lemon.

SAUCE FOR SWEET PUDDINGS

Cream two ounces of butter, add two ounces of castor sugar, cream again and add by degrees a wineglassful of brandy or rum, with a tablespoonful of hot milk or water. Stir till thoroughly mixed, and either pour round the pudding or serve in a sauce-boat.

SCHAUM SAUCE

4 egg yolks; 2 oz. sugar; 1 glass sherry or brandy; lemon juice and peel; salt; 1 dessertsp. cream.

Put the egg yolks in a small deep stewpan; add the sifted sugar, the sherry or brandy, a little lemon juice and grated peel, and a grain of salt. A dessertspoonful of cream may be added. Whisk the sauce over a moderate heat, taking care to set the saucepan which contains the mixture in another of larger size, in which is a full inch depth of hot water. As soon as it is a well-set creamy sauce, pour it into a very hot silver sauce-boat or over the pudding.

SEA FOAM SAUCE

3 level dessertsp. butter; 3 level dessertsp. flour; 4 oz. sugar; 1 egg; 1 tsp. vanilla essence.

Cream the butter and gradually add the flour first mixed with the sugar, stirring all the time. Now add a well-beaten egg yolk, a teacupful of water and the vanilla essence, and cook in a double saucepan until thick. Let this cool, and just before serving, add the stiffly whisked white of an egg.

SENIOR WRANGLER SAUCE

Hard Sauce (p. 203) flavoured with brandy or sherry, to which a few ground almonds have been added.

SILVERY SAUCE (Créole)

8 oz. sugar; 1 tbs. butter; 1 pint milk; 2 egg whites; lemon or vanilla flavouring.

Cream the sugar with the butter. Set the milk to boil, and as soon as it begins to simmer, add the creamed butter and sugar. Let all simmer gently for a few minutes, then take it from the fire, and add the egg whites whipped to a stiff froth. Then add lemon or vanilla flavouring to taste and serve hot or cold.

STRAWBERRY SAUCE 1

Strawberry-jam purée diluted with syrup to taste and flavoured with Kirsch.

STRAWBERRY SAUCE 2

Cream eight ounces of sugar and four ounces of butter, then add the whisked white of an egg and one pound of strawberries, chopped or mashed. This sauce should be left on ice for several hours before serving.

SWEET SAUCE 1 (English)

Make a White Sauce with an ounce of butter, half an ounce of flour and half a pint of milk. Sweeten with one or two ounces of sugar. Finish with another ounce of butter in little pieces and a dash of vanilla flavouring.

SWEET SAUCE 2

Mix a teaspoonful of arrowroot or cornflour smoothly with a little water. Then stir it into a quarter of a pint of boiling milk. Cook, stirring, for five minutes, then add an ounce of sugar, the flavouring chosen (any of the commercial flavouring essences), and finish with half an ounce of butter.

TINNED FRUIT SAUCE

In moments of serious emergency, the juice from a tin of fruit will often make quite a good hot sauce, if thickened with a little arrowroot and further flavoured, when possible, with a spoonful or two of a suitable liqueur.

VANILLA SAUCE 1

This is a Cornflour (p. 200) or a sweet Melted-Butter Sauce (p. 96), flavoured with vanilla and often enriched by a liaison of egg yolk.

VANILLA SAUCE 2

½ tbs. potato flour or arrowroot; 1 pint milk; 1 tbs. castor sugar; vanilla flavouring or 1 vanilla pod; 2 egg yolks.

Mix the potato flour or arrowroot with a little of the milk and when it is quite smooth add the rest of the milk. Put this into a double saucepan with the castor sugar, a few drops of vanilla flavouring or, better, a vanilla pod, and the egg yolks. Beat together and stir, slowly bringing nearly to the boil. Strain through a fine sieve before it boils, and continue to stir while the sauce cools to prevent a skin from forming. Serve cold.

WHIPPED CUSTARD SAUCE

Make a Custard (p. 200) with an egg yolk and half a pint of milk, sweetening and flavouring it to taste. Then whisk the white stiffly, add it to the Custard and heat again until it is light and frothy, whisking all the time. Serve immediately.

WINE SAUCE 1 (English)

lemon rind; 1½ oz. sugar; 1 oz. butter; good ½ tsp. flour; 1½ wineglass sherry, Madeira or sweet white wine.

Boil together for a quarter of an hour a wineglassful of water, the very thinly cut rind of half a small lemon and about an ounce and a half of sugar. Then take out the lemon peel and stir in the butter previously kneaded with the flour. When the sauce is smooth, add the sherry, Madeira or other suitable sweet white wine, and just heat up for a moment before serving.

WINE SAUCE 2

Make half a pint of Melted-Butter Sauce (p. 96), add a glass of sherry and a tablespoonful of castor sugar.

WINE SAUCE 3

Mix some wine gradually with a tablespoonful of flour, using a glassful in all. When smoothly mixed, let this boil for five minutes, then add a quarter of an ounce of butter and a tablespoonful of brown sugar, and pass through a strainer to serve hot.

YANKEE SAUCE

4 oz. butter; 10 oz. icing sugar; 3 level tsp. cornflour; 1 tsp. vinegar; 1½ tsp. vanilla essence.

Cream the butter with the icing sugar. Mix the cornflour with two tablespoonfuls of cold water and add this by degrees to half a pint of boiling water, boiling until it clears. Then, stirring quickly, add the first mixture, and flavour with the vinegar and vanilla essence.

YELLOW SAUCE

Beat two eggs until they are light, then add gradually six ounces of sugar, beating all the time. Flavour with a teaspoonful of brandy or vanilla essence.

Index

218

Index

Index

Index